The Good Entrepreneur

Cristina Santini

The Good Entrepreneur

Mapping the Role of Entrepreneurship in Society

palgrave
macmillan

Cristina Santini
San Raffaele University of Rome
Rome, Italy

ISBN 978-3-030-59331-5 ISBN 978-3-030-59332-2 (eBook)
https://doi.org/10.1007/978-3-030-59332-2

This Palgrave Macmillan imprint is published by the registered company Springer Nature Switzerland AG
The registered company address is: Gewerbestrasse 11, 6330 Cham, Switzerland

Introduction

Over the years, we have seen that ethical components have gained relevancy in the decision-making process. Social motives, green and ecological awareness, and sustainable orientation have inspired new start-ups or have reshaped existing businesses. Some questions emerge in entrepreneurship and deal with doing well by doing good, or doing well and doing good. The concept of entrepreneurship and entrepreneur has evolved since its introduction. New issues have attracted scholarly interest and new topics and research questions have emerged. The concepts of doing well and the idea of good have changed.

New types of entrepreneurs have emerged and research niches were born; they aim to explore the relationship between personal commitment, ethical motives and traditional traits of entrepreneurship. This book focuses on the good entrepreneur: it explores the relationship between entrepreneurs and the pursuit of good and it examines the evolution of research in the field.

The book starts with the evolution of entrepreneurship. The first chapter explores how the research field on entrepreneurship has evolved since the introduction of the theme.

It highlights the drivers that promote research in entrepreneurship, and the steps and features that characterise its development, from the debate to the legitimacy of the field to the progressive fragmentation of research. The chapter introduces the topic of research niche development within entrepreneurship: this introduces to further exploration of different types of entrepreneurs, social, green, environmental, sustainable entrepreneur and ecopreneur, in the following chapters.

The second chapter focuses on the issue of good and the pursuit of good by entrepreneurs. It explores what it means for an entrepreneur to pursue the good and it shows how the relationship entrepreneur-good has evolved over the years. Initially, the pursuit of good was an element far from the business culture; today, with the advent of new business models, and the changing of markets and society, managers and entrepreneurs show a growing interest for what is good. We discuss the concept of good in entrepreneurship and what it means to be a good entrepreneur. We explore the motivation that fosters an interest for doing good in entrepreneurs; we highlight the role of environmental factors and personal motivations.

Chapters 3 and 4 focus on the types of good entrepreneurs. We talk about some emerging research niches, and we explore the typologies of social entrepreneur, green, environmental, sustainable and ecopreneur. Here, we aim to highlight the dynamics that lead to the birth of niches and to explore what are the features of these selected types of entrepreneurs.

The last chapter proposes a reflection with a mainly academic perspective: our aim is to find out the phases of a research niche and publications trends. We provide an overview of strengths and weaknesses of the bibliometric approach in the evaluation of the literature. After having discussed the role of grey literature for the birth of research niches, we provide an analysis of research trends of the selected types of entrepreneurs.

This book aims to stimulate questions about entrepreneurship: What does it mean today for an entrepreneur to be good and to pursue the good? What will be the future scenario for scholars who deal with the issue of good entrepreneur and entrepreneurship in general?

Contents

List of Figures

List of Tables

CHAPTER 1

The Evolution of Entrepreneurship

Abstract The research field of entrepreneurship is vast, and it attracts scholars from different disciplines. The chapter provides an overview of the evolution of entrepreneurship, and it highlights the drivers that have contributed to the growth of the domain. In this chapter, we also focus on the debate upon the legitimacy of entrepreneurship. After having analysed the different stages of the life cycle of a research field and having discussed the maturity of the thematic, we introduce the concept of research niche, and we point out future trends and evolution of academic literature on entrepreneurship.

Keywords Entrepreneurship · Research drivers · Legitimacy · Research life cycle · Maturity · Research niche

Introduction

The study of the evolution of entrepreneurship has attracted many scholars from different disciplines. The entrepreneurship field is most dynamic in management and social science (Audretsch, 2012); its development is somehow astonishing, since a few decades ago it was "sparse, virtually non-existent; it was mostly irrelevant" (Audretsch, 2012: 755).

C. Santini, *The Good Entrepreneur*,
https://doi.org/10.1007/978-3-030-59332-2_1

From a first analysis of the distribution of theoretical contributions to the field, we can say that the issue has attracted scholars from business, management, economics and environmental studies.[1]

A sort of dualism characterises entrepreneurship: on one side the individualistic pressure and on the other the need for the development of a scientific field (Aldrich & Howard, 2012).

Academicians in the entrepreneurial field have been able to establish a long career in many prestigious universities (Aldrich & Howard, 2012; Landstrom, Harirchi, & Astrom, 2012) and to create groups of scholars that have focused on some specific issues.

The debate on the field of entrepreneurship is endless. In a paper published in 1996, Harrison and Leitch describe the typical situation that scholars in entrepreneurship must face.

> We are asked 'What is do you do?' and we reply 'I'm a professor of entrepreneurship' or 'I'm an entrepreneurship researcher.' Almost invariably, this provokes the follow-up question 'What is entrepreneurship?' or 'What exactly do you do?' which asks us to define, explain and characterize our subject. This is not, it must be noted, a situation faced by others: for example, pilots, teachers of physics, or students or medicine do not usually go through this question-and-answer session. (Harrison & Leitch, 1996, p. 66)

To define entrepreneurship is extremely difficult; to define what researchers in entrepreneurship do is even more arduous.

In this chapter, our aim is to describe how entrepreneurship has evolved as a research field. We also want to outline what are the drivers that have promoted research in this field. In our vision, the understanding of the reasons behind academic interests towards some theoretical issues can help evaluate future trends and development. What follows is a fascinating journey in cultural and economic changes seen through the lens of research in entrepreneurship.

[1] From a preliminary research carried on WOS database, we have observed that out of a total of 1305 records related to the topic "Evolution of Entrepreneurship" in the period 1996–2020 (limited to the first term of 2020), 556 were belonging to the "business" area, 541 to the "management" area and 241 to the Economics area; 77 were belonging to the field regional urban planning.

Drivers

Research in entrepreneurship is in continuous evolution; it is not only growing by dimension, but also by "coverage" or, in other words, by thematic issues. In the literature, the question "where is research in entrepreneurship going?" often emerges. Boshoff, Bennett and Owusu (1992) in the early 1990s have explored the present and future directions of research in the field. The authors, as well as other scholars—see, for example, Bruton, Ahlstrom and Li (2008), Coombs, Sadrieh and Annavarjula (2009), Bruton, Ahlstrom, and Li (2010) or Macke, Sarate, Domeneghini, Silva, and Da (2018)—have investigated the development of research in entrepreneurship with the aim of understanding phases, trends and future directions. Each contribution reflects the scholars' approach, the scope of the study and the background theory.

Several drivers promote a change in entrepreneurship and, as a consequence, they influence scholarly research in the field. There is no doubt that the changes that take place in the industry contribute to transforming the features of entrepreneurship (Agarwal & Braguinsky, 2015). Some scholars have explored the relationship between industry characteristics and entrepreneurship; in some cases, the presence of small companies promotes the growth of entrepreneurs' population (Carlsson et al., 2013). Nevertheless, some characteristics of the industry can foster or inhibit entrepreneurial behaviour: barriers to entrance, financial resources or technological development can dissuade start-uppers or new entrants (Lofstrom, Bates, & Parker, 2014).

Changes in society and technology have revolutionised the features of entrepreneurship: the digitalisation process has created new paths for entrepreneurs (Landstrom, 2020).

For instance, the opportunities created by the web and digital economy have represented a breeding ground for e-entrepreneurs, who focus on the development of e-commerce companies (Matlay, 2004). At the same time, the development of web-based relationships and networks has reshaped the characteristics of entrepreneurs—or e-entrepreneurs—who had to develop specific skills.

Yet, universities have a leading role in creating the conditions for a change in entrepreneurship and its promotion among students (Link, Siegel, & Wright, 2015). There is no doubt that educational institutions focusing on entrepreneurship stimulate new venture creations (Gerosa & Tirapani, 2013). Furthermore, the recognition of the proactive role of educational institutions in promoting entrepreneurial development has nurtured the attention for this type of programmes that have received financial support from institutions, associations or government.

The literature examines the phenomenon of evolution in entrepreneurship. Among the various contributions, we summarise the work by Landstrom (2020) that clearly outlines evolutionary paths in entrepreneurship. What we can observe is a fluid research field where new topics progressively grow.

Entrepreneurship, as a research area, strongly emerged in the seventies.

Landstrom (2020) highlights five periods in research: "the forerunners in mainstream disciplines, the formation of the field, the growth of entrepreneurship research, the golden era, and finally, the establishment of a scholarly field in its own right" (p. 1).

The life cycle of entrepreneurship described by Landstrom (2020) shows the journey of this research field: researchers initially have to strive for attracting scholars interest and for achieving support for their research. Then, scholars concentrate their efforts on disseminating findings and on stimulating an academic debate; they aim at increasing research in entrepreneurship. When a topic achieves notoriety than the number of publications that deal with the issue grows, the final step is the full recognition of a scholarly field of study.

The process of recognition of entrepreneurship as a scholarly field is challenging: background research shows that positive outcomes of entrepreneurship have attracted the interest of academicians and institutions. As an example, we can think about the relationship between entrepreneurs and small business.

The recognised importance of the role of entrepreneurship in the flourishing of small businesses and start-ups has nurtured research: entrepreneurship, seen as one of the critical drivers for job creation (Boshoff, Bennett, & Owusu, 1992), has found support and encouragement not only from academics but also from institutions. Institutions and policymakers gained awareness about the role of entrepreneurship for revitalising the job market and promoting local development. In other words, supporting entrepreneurship means for governments to sustain local communities through job creation.

Thus, changes are happening at all levels of society and involve many types of organisations: an example—previously outlined—concerns the digitalisation of markets. Education changed, too: new needs emerge from communities, and they stimulate not only research but also educational programmes.

The change itself of the academic and university landscape outlines the importance of researching in the field of entrepreneurship. The development of some research and educational programmes over the last two decades confirms the changes occurring in the Higher Education System. The revolution that is taking place at a global level is clearly described by Etzkowitz (2001), who writes: "Universities have become engines of regional economic development, developing new organisational mechanisms for this purpose as well as for the conservation, extension and dissemination of knowledge. Opportunities to translate research into industrial applications were always present, yet few academics took advantage of them. The few who did were a distinct and unusual minority" (p. 19).

Concepts like "third mission" or "fourth mission" progressively gained importance in the vision of Educational Systems. One of the aims of universities is to contribute to local development, to make knowledge accessible and to promote research that answers industrial needs.

It is easy to understand why education blinked its eye to entrepreneurship; yet designing entrepreneurial educational programmes require in-depth knowledge about entrepreneurship. As a consequence, the need to educate to entrepreneurship has stimulated research in the field.

There is another factor that has promoted research in entrepreneurship: in some countries, the cultural system supports entrepreneurial development and entrepreneurship.

In Northern America, for example, entrepreneurs have been considered as part of the local culture: Boshoff et al. (1992) underline that entrepreneurs in the USA are part of the *American Dream*. Under this perspective, research in entrepreneurship explores a subject that is part of the local culture, and that proposes a successful model.

There is no doubt that entrepreneurship plays a central role in the development of communities.

In an article published by Santini et al. (2011), we find evidence of the importance given by Chinese immigrant enclaves to entrepreneurship: workers that become entrepreneurs achieve a position in the local community. In the specific case of Chinese immigrant entrepreneurs, there is an intense relationship with the country of origin, the culture and the set of norms and beliefs that inspire the vision of entrepreneurship.[2]

Entrepreneurs can also be developing and changing agents: in areas where there is a need for economic and cultural development, entrepreneurs can represent an opportunity for local communities. We can think about rural areas or poor and disadvantaged neighbourhoods; in these cases, there is a positive perception of entrepreneurs.

The general appreciation for this type of actors stimulates in academics an interest in research projects on entrepreneurship.

The dissemination of findings is facilitated when scholars find responsiveness in the audience: people who think, for cultural reasons, that entrepreneurs personify self-fulfilment are favourably disposed to welcome research inputs.

In general, we can say that the relevancy of entrepreneurship has grown all over the world.

The recognition of entrepreneurial social responsibility in the development of a country's wealth has fostered a positive perception of entrepreneurs. Consequently, research in entrepreneurship has increased.

Legitimacy

Entrepreneurship got the legitimacy to be recognised as a scientific discipline with its rights starting from the 1970s to 1980s; the contributions emerging from various fields have made of this research issue a multifaceted topic that is particularly open to cross-fertilisation.

Scholars (Landstrom, 2020) have underlined the importance of investigating the social role covered by the entrepreneurial research field, rather than focusing on its intellectual development.

For what concerns the legitimation process, we must underline one aspect.

[2] In the cited article, the authors depict the process that leaded Chinese immigrants in the city of Prato (in Tuscany, Italy) to become entrepreneurs. The city, once one of the leading industrial districts for fashion and textile production, hosts one of the biggest Chinese communities in Italy and Europe. Prato has witnessed a growth in the number of Chinese entrepreneurs; their evolution from immigrant workers to entrepreneurs shows the influence of the "laoban" concept (laoban literally means "boss") that directly derives from Chinese culture.

Legitimacy is a word that we have frequently encountered in our research. There is an extensive academic debate about the lack of legitimacy in the field of entrepreneurship.

During the investigation on the development of entrepreneurship, we have observed that scholars put many efforts into understanding how this research field has evolved. Scholars need to follow trends and research directions not only because they need to monitor research progression, but also because they need to legitimate this field of study (Chandra & Lozano, 2018). Therefore, the exploration of the evolution of a research field contributes to its legitimation process.

Legitimation is fruitful for scholars, and it also has some practical implications (Busenitz et al., 2003): among academics, there is an association between legitimacy and autonomy, power recognition and publication success.

Legitimation has the power to open the doors to scholars not only in terms of academic recognition: we can now fully understand the relevance of the debate on legitimacy.

Defining what legitimacy is an arduous task, and it is much easier to find a description of the purposes of legitimacy (see, for example, Jané, Van Esch, & Bilimoria, 2018).

Generally speaking, legitimacy is an evaluation (Jané, Van Esch, & Bilimoria, 2018).

Suchman (1995) provides a fascinating reflection upon the process and the role of legitimacy in the research and academic system.

Suchman (1995) observes that legitimacy is a generalised perception; it suggests that the actions of an entity are desirable. Once legitimated, actions are appropriate within some socially constructed system of norms, values, beliefs and definitions. Legitimacy under this perspective represents a sort of endorsement, since it ensures the implicit approval of actions, given their alignment to a set of values.

The definition mentioned above comes from the organisational theory, and it depicts the idea of consensus built around a concept, a theory or, as some scholars say (Kuhn, 1962), an academic paradigm. There is a mutual relationship between the establishment of a theoretical paradigm and legitimacy (Kuhn, 1962). The concepts of commonalities and sharing are at the base of the definition of any conceptual model (Onwuegbuzie, Johnson, & Collins, 2011); also, the establishment of collaborations among academicians improves the reputation of discipline.

Collaboration among scholars not only fosters the advances in knowledge (Howard & Aldrich, 2012), but it also shows that academicians agree on the importance of researching the same topic.

Also, Busenitz et al. (2003) provide a definition of legitimacy applied to the field of entrepreneurial research: "With legitimacy we mean the extent to which research in entrepreneurship advances useful knowledge and is substantively endorsed by powerful external collective actors" (p. 286). Again, endorsement and value recognition provide value to research: the more the system of beliefs, constructs and convictions is approved and shared by an audience, the more it is capable of legitimate itself and to attract resources. Vice versa, delegitimisation can happen. For what concerns the academic context, several factors can obstacle the legitimation process of a research field: for example, adverse outcomes for the production and dissemination of knowledge reduce a positive evaluation of legitimacy (Jané et al., 2018). Under-legitimation can happen because of many reasons: there can be, for example, a value incongruence with the dominant academic community. In this case, research topics can show a misalignment with what expressed and shared by the scholarly community or their research topic can have some inequity issues. There is another element in the analysis by Jané et al. (2018) that seized our attention. According to the authors, if under-represented and under-valued scholars populate a research field, a threat arises for its legitimation. This consideration opens to multiple questions: How can we assess the value of a scholar? How can we define the degree of representativeness of a scholar? Bibliometric indexes can provide information. Thus, a system that evaluates scholars' impact by adopting a bibliometric approach can have flaws. Furthermore, the article introduces other "problems": scholars that study the research topic can be at the centre of a delegitimation process. As we can see, the problem becomes more and more complicated.

The adoption of a legitimation strategy is vital for the achievement of legitimacy (Suchman, 1995). By observing in particular business schools, it emerges which measures can improve legitimacy (Jané et al., 2018): to adopt of a positivist approach to science; to underline quantitative methodology when designing research programmes; or to attract academics from prestigious institutions. The relationship between creating a consensus and achieving legitimacy becomes clear.

Talking about the legitimation of entrepreneurship is somehow strange: we are referring to a research field that appears vivid, prolific and that attracts scholars from various disciplines to establish a dialogue and to develop cross contaminations.

Among some scholars (Low, 2001; Busenitz et al., 2003), it is a common thought that such research field is still in search of legitimacy: Low (2001) when talking about research in entrepreneurship describes a flurry of activities that boosted the attention towards the area. However, he highlights the "modest level of academic legitimacy". The reason behind this difficulty in achieving legitimacy is because of the nature itself of entrepreneurship (Low, 2001). Also defining entrepreneurship is extremely difficult (Low, 2001; Low & Macmillan, 1988); the continuous overlapping of constructs (Low & Macmillan, 1988) can improve the difficulties in achieving academic legitimation.

Defining Phases

The interest in classifying and in performing analysis of scholarly contributions has grown (Westbrook, 1994). Entrepreneurship is an endless research field, where new topics and issues emerge as society evolves. Dealing with entrepreneurship is complicated, due to the emerging of a different approach and the impressive numbers of publications available. It is worth focusing on the answer to: "how did we get here?". Understanding the evolution of the research field, and more specifically its phases, can be particularly helpful.

In general, we observe that the analysis of research trends has spread among many fields, even thanks to the availability of some analysis tools widely employed in other disciplines. For example, the Library and Information Science (LIS) has created a breeding ground for the implementation of analytical tools and for a research approach that examines "the numbers" of scholars' publications.

Many scholars employ bibliometric also for measuring the impact of a paper, and we can understand even what role an author had in the development of a research topic (Cobo, López-Herrera, Herrera-Viedma, & Herrera, 2011). We must highlight that bibliometric analysis has encountered many critics. In particular, some authors have underlined that scholars' evaluation often happens independently from the context; research institutes are part of the community, and the size of a research institute—that is related to the number of scholars that belong to the institution—can influence the diffusion of knowledge. The work by (Tol,

2012) underlines the limits and challenges of a bibliometric approach, and offers useful inputs for further reflections.

There is a fascinating article published by Gartner, Davidsson, and Zahra (2006) that stimulated our reflection on the importance of citations and research impact.

The distribution of publications, in general, shows a trend of a low degree of concentration. In other words, the vast majority of scholars have only one or two publications, and quite few publish more than one article in their field. Furthermore, there is a trend that reinforces the visibility of one paper: once a document has been cited, it is more likely to be mentioned again. Those papers which have gained notoriety among scholars will experiment a growth in citations. The article by Gartner et al. dates back to 2006, but some insights, although research in entrepreneurship has grown, are still valid in our opinion. First of all, we confirm that some scholars show strong linkages with other disciplines, such as psychology, economics or sociology. Second, we agree with the authors when they explain that "the field is shaped not by those who tell others what to do, but by those who conduct interesting research that attracts a following" (p. 327).

Many published articles aim to understand the distribution of research over time, the impact—in terms, for example, of citations—and the correlation among citations or the diffusion of some terms or keywords.

In work published in 2018, Chandra proposes two research questions: "how has the entrepreneurship as a field of research changed over time? What are the latest trends in terms of new and highly cited topics in the field?".

The field of entrepreneurship shows, with the help of bibliometric analysis, a dynamic scenario: over time, some topics appear, others disappear, and some issues remain as milestones over time.[3]

[3] In this paragraph, we refer to "bibliometric analysis" (Cobo et al., 2011) provide the following definition of bibliometrics: "bibliometrics is a set of methods used to study or measure texts and information, especially in big datasets. Many research fields use bibliometric methods to explore the impact of their field, the impact of a set of researchers, or the impact of a particular paper (Henderson, Shurville, & Fernstrom, 2009; van Raan, 2005). In bibliometrics, there are two main procedures: performance analysis and science mapping (Noyons, Moed, & Luwel, 1999; van Raan, 2005). Performance analysis aims at evaluating groups of scientific actors (countries, universities, depart- ments, researchers) and the impact of their activity (Noyons, et al., 1999; van Raan, 2005) on the basis of bibliographic data. Science mapping aims at displaying the structural and dynamic aspects of scientific research (Börner, Chen, & Boyack, 2003; Noyons et al., 1999). A science

From background literature, it appears that research in entrepreneurship covers many issues; with its evolution over time, new topics came out, and the attention of scholars focused on some specific research themes.

Scholars—attracted by new and promising themes—have moved their attention to something new to them, or related to the covered issues. Eminent scholars have dedicated time and efforts to develop publications that explore problems that are expected to have a forthcoming impact in terms of research outcomes. Younger researchers have seen in innovative issues a mean for getting a differentiation from the larger population of academicians and achieve visibility through publications.

Several authors have tried to depict the steps of research in entrepreneurship by underlining the main trends. Among the various papers, we have focused on the work published by Chandra and Lozano (2018): they employ science mapping and represent a clear example of what we have depicted above.

Initially, at the beginning of the 1990s, academic attention focused on the role of personality traits of entrepreneurs; research was person-centric (Chandra & Lozano, 2018). Later, there was more attention to the definition of the field and some issues such as the relationship with innovation or entrepreneurial process and opportunity recognition.

Research has shown development in peer-reviewed journals in the early 2000, and in the period 2008–2013, new issues emerged, such as social entrepreneurship, business ethics, corporate social responsibility or employment and job creation (Chandra & Lozano, 2018).

The rising of the interest in ethics, social and employment reveals that research tries to answer to problems that affect society. Further on, we will see that the increasing attention of institution and organisations for societal issues has created the condition for the growth of entrepreneurial research in this area.

Fragmentation

When reading the literature on entrepreneurship, one of the most diffused words is "fragmented". Some authors talk about accumulative fragmentation (Busenitz et al., 2003).

map is used to represent the cognitive structure of a research field" (p. 146). The cited article describes the aims and the tools of bibliometric analysis.

This status of fragmentation is seen as an obstacle for entrepreneurship to gain a developed disciplinary status in a science framework (Aldrich & Howard, 2012).

Where this fragmentation arises?

The high permeability of boundaries of the discipline fosters fragmentation (Busenitz et al., 2003): scholars from different disciplines and various field of research when applying their insights and concepts to the entrepreneurial settings improve fragmentation.

Nevertheless, the multifaceted nature of entrepreneurship is under everybody's eyes: the capability of entrepreneurship to attract scholars from different fields contributed to make it a meta-field (Reader & Watkins, 2006). The existence of a collaborative network among scholars from various disciplines has created a breeding ground not only for cross-fertilisation but also for the diffusion of articles among academic journals from multiple fields.

The above-described scenario has contributed to the diffusion of the discipline and its growth by revealing the importance covered by the issue in different fields. Still, it also brought an improvement in the number of articles published in non-specific journals.

The rapid growth of scholarly output has fostered the complexity and heterogeneity of research (Audretsch, 2012). There is an enhancement of the degree of fragmentation: different scholars' academic tradition and multiple approaches create a vivid, complex puzzle that it is still evolving.

Nevertheless, some scholars may see in fragmentation an inhibitor of signs of progress in the discipline (Aldrich & Baker, 1997).

Given this complicated situation, it is challenging to realize a comprehensive picture of the different areas of interest cover by entrepreneurship. Many scholars have tried to define how entrepreneurship has developed, but, as outlined by Ferreira, Reis, and Miranda (2015), this field "is still far from well mapped and understood" (p. 2).

To give an idea of how entrepreneurship is available in many categories, we have performed a simple analysis of keywords by exploring the Web of Science (WOS) database. We have searched for documents which contain "entrepreneurship" as a topic in a wide range of time (1945–2020). Results were impressive: 55406 works published in the WOS database, and the most consistent category of documents is "article journal". We have then analysed the published articles that appear in the WOS database in the considered period. It is interesting to note that the ten leading journals emerging for the number of published articles are: *Sustainability*; *Journal of Cleaner Production; Small Business Economics*; *Journal of Business Ethics*; *Technological Forecasting and Social Change*; *Journal of Business Research*; *Entrepreneurship Theory and Practice*; *Journal of Business Venturing*; *Research Policies*; *Organisation Studies.*

Yet, the publication trend shows a high degree of fragmentation, since the most active journal in publishing accounts for 2.38% of publication and entrepreneurship theory and practice for 1.121% of the total. When we observe the number of articles published in the last ten years, we can see a growth: the trend has always been positive, from 200 articles published in 2011, to 4224 in 2018 and 5680 in 2019. The most active journal in publishing articles that contain the topic "entrepreneurship" seems to be sustainability. Yet, the proliferation of printed materials is connected somehow to the birth of new academic journals with open access and capable of publishing a considerable number of issues per year. The growth of open access journals has reshaped the academic orientation towards publishing decisions (Noorden, 2013). Open access publishing is conventional in mathematical or physics, and it is slowly getting a diffusion in social science (Pincock, 2013). Open access publishing has been promoted by educational institutions which in some cases require authors to make their work more accessible (Pincock, 2013). Given the scenario, there is no doubt about the existence of favourable conditions for the birth of new open access journals that can include such topics as entrepreneurship.

We must underline an aspect: this number-based approach shows some limitations. Counting up the articles that contain the topic "entrepreneurship" only provides a partial view of the phenomenon. Mitchell (2011) examines the growth of the domain of entrepreneurship research. He observes two indicators that are employed for assessing the dynamism of research: the number of articles that use the term "entrepreneurship" published on A and A- journals and the number of faculty members that became members of the Entrepreneurship Division of the Academy of Management. He underlines the limits of this approach that "does not fully explain the increasing-returns phenomenon in entrepreneurship research, but it provides a starting place and some relevant indicators. Thus, assuming differences in scholarly interests, and the capability of the peer review process to inhibit direct duplication (as distinct from replication), these basic counts do illustrate how the increasing breadth of thinking and scholarship brought to entrepreneurship research by these many more articles written by many more scholars, demonstrates the phenomenon of the increasing return at work: a growing "positive" feedback momentum due to self-reinforcement" (p. 618).

We don't want to provide a comment of literature review in the field, even because any possible taxonomy of entrepreneurship depends on the scholar's theoretical approach.

The work by Kuratko and Morris (2018) clearly outlines some specialty areas; according to this paper, research in the field focuses on selected themes such as opportunities and the entrepreneurial process; venture financing; entrepreneurial cognition; economic development and entrepreneurship; family business; corporate entrepreneurship; social entrepreneurship and sustainability; women and minority entrepreneurship; global entrepreneurship; and entrepreneurship research, education and pedagogy. Differently from what Kuratko and Morris (2018) did, some other scholars have tried to employ bibliometric analysis for understanding the trajectories of research in entrepreneurship, to classify the "fragments" of the discipline.

The implementation of bibliometric studies has contributed to increasing the number of publications in the field.

Ferreira et al. (2015) show that the number of published articles increases with the availability of financial support and the birth of new research centres; indeed, there are a limited number of eminent scholars, whose role in the development of research is pivotal, according to the insights that emerge from co-citation analysis. The attention given to some issues varies over time, and some themes might emerge in specific periods; this complicates further definitions of the state of the art of research themes in the discipline.

To give an idea of the taxonomies and fragmentation of entrepreneurship, we provide some examples in the literature in Table 1.1.

We clearly understand that to provide a definition and classification is challenging. Scholars' approach influences without any doubts results and publication strategy. Given the complexity of the circumstance and the lack of accepted categorisation of streams of entrepreneurship research, we understand those who suggest that no distinctive stream exists (Schildt, Zahra, & Sillanpää, 2006).

Table 1.1 Research themes in entrepreneurship (bibliometric based classification)

Research themes	*Source*
Entrepreneurial process; environmental and external determinants of entrepreneurship; value creation and performance; methods, theories and research issues; psychological, cognitive and individual characteristics; entrepreneurial networks; high-tech entrepreneurship; corporate venturing and business competition; entrepreneurial opportunities; etc	Ferreira et al. (2015)
Institutions and institutional entrepreneurship; innovation and technology management; policy and development; entrepreneurial process and opportunities; new ventures; person-centric issues; family business and management team	Chandra and Lozano (2018)
Entrepreneurship, network, culture, success, succession, agency cost, venture, embeddedness, firm, business, ownership structure, corporate governance, conceptual issues, consequence, dynamic, exploratory evidence, household, industry, and wealth.[5]	(López-Fernández, Serrano-Bedia, & Pérez-Pérez, 2016)
Leadership and top management teams; organisational decision-making theory; organisational learning and problem-solving; external triggers of industrial change, exploration, and entrepreneurship; survival of firm; institutions and institutional entrepreneurship; top management characteristics and success; searching for the essence of entrepreneurship; liabilities of newness and survival mechanisms; knowledge-based view of the firm; trust and relational capital; risk-taking among entrepreneurs; environmental determinants of entrepreneurial success; statistical methodology; high-tech entrepreneurship	(Schildt, Zahra, & Sillanpää, 2006)

Maturity

It is tough to determine which phase research is encountering. For what concerns entrepreneurship, the evaluation of the stage of the "research life cycle" is even harder, since there is not a consensus among scholars (Chandra & Lozano, 2018).

The concept of a life cycle, if applied to research, is made up by several stages: in the first stage, the research issue appears new to academicians; as the interest towards the research issue arises, original papers are released, and there is a growth in the number of publications. In the earliest stage of the life cycle, scholars focus on methodology and try to highlight findings that are susceptible to generalisation. One of the scholar's aims in the earliest stage of discipline is to achieve legitimacy; researchers try to capture people's attention and to foster a consensus around the research issues. Since the research field has reached its maturity, there has been a wide diffusion of the topic, and a vast majority of academics in the area have familiarity with the proposed research issues.

In our attempt to define the state of the art of research in entrepreneurship, we have encountered the adjective "mature" in many published papers. It is not unusual to read that entrepreneurship is a mature research field. This is disorienting scholars: if research in entrepreneurship is growing, how can we say that it is mature?

Generally speaking, the concept of maturity in people's mind finds an association with steady growth and the beginning of the decline. Research on entrepreneurship is experiencing growing trends.

Under what circumstances scholars define a research field as mature? What are the main signals of maturity? In social science and management, maturity is associated with a life cycle stage that follows a period of growth. When an organisation or a product reaches its maturity, its growth rate is not so high as in the previous phases, and a revitalisation strategy often takes place.

Yet, the term "maturity" is often associated with a negative perception. Borrowing some insights from the literature that focuses on the maturity assessment models, and more specifically from the article by Mettler (2011), we can evaluate the degree of maturity of a research field, by observing the process, the object or people's capability.

In other words, when the process of knowledge creation—in this case—is explicitly defined, managed and controlled, we can say that we are in front of a mature process.

When analysing the degree of "sophistication" of output, we can stand in front of a signal of maturity. Finally, when people are enabled to create knowledge, this means that we are observing a mature phenomenon.

This short reflection upon the meaning of maturity underlines the positive sense of being mature.

Under this perspective, there is no doubt that entrepreneurship is a mature research field, capable of producing knowledge and findings. Yet, for many scholars, being mature means being near the point of having a few left to say.

It is interesting to understand what are the signals of maturity.

Some authors have underlined how research in entrepreneurship was getting into a maturity phase (Cornelius, Landstrom, & Persson, 2006) since it was becoming internally oriented and self-centred. The arising of "research circles"—as defined by Cornelius et al. (2006)—was emerging as one of the consequences of the evolution of the research field. Some authors have observed that the grouping of research was progressively forming some clusters (Cornelius et al., 2006) and this is evidence of maturity, since it contributes to improving the degree of specialisation in the field.

Katz (2008) recovers the positive association maturity, entrepreneurship, when he writes: "Foremost, maturity means that the discipline has come to some agreement on its identity, meaning, and pedagogically, what needs to be taught".

As it can be argued, it is not easy to define how to establish the degree of maturity, and it is even harder to find insights that specifically refer to models that predict the degree of maturity in a research field. Authors employ categories used by academics when exploring some specific issues for understanding the maturity phase of entrepreneurship. In this direction, Katz (2008) suggests, by borrowing the categories of the business life cycle, to consider as a signal of maturity in entrepreneurship: "Having a little need for a product design emphasis, having a low to moderate market growth rate, and having a large number of segments or niches" (p. 553).

The convergence around a set of standards in this research field has contributed to reducing the need for newer approaches or "design" in the discipline.[6] For what concerns the growth rate, it is hard to say that the growth has been steady. The investigation carried by Hlady-Rispal & Jouison-Laffitte (2014) shows that the number of articles published in academic journals grew in the last decade; yet, since "entrepreneurship is everywhere" (Katz, 2008), it is hard to say if this trend is confirmed or

[6] In the paper, Katz (2008) specifically refers to courses in entrepreneurship, but the emerging insights can be generalized and they can be applied to the domain of entrepreneurship.

not. What we can say is that there are both an ongoing fragmentation and the emerging of niches in the field.

From Fragments to Niches

We have previously outlined how research in entrepreneurship is fragmented. Therefore, some "fragments" have evolved and became niches.

In our view, the evolution of research in entrepreneurship follows a development by niches. There is a difference between a niche and a fragment. Generally speaking, a fragment is as part of a whole.

According to the Oxford Dictionary, a fragment can be defined as an "Isolated or incomplete part".

The definition for niche, in the Oxford Dictionary, is "a comfortable or suitable position in life or employment". When referring to business, a niche is "a specialised but profitable corner of the market" (Oxford dictionary).

When we think about niches, the first impression is that they are comfortable and profitable; they are a narrowed space that is carved out from a mass. Playing in a niche means to operate in a sheltered place, where the degree of competition is lower.

When we think about fragments, instead, the first concept that comes to our mind is "separation".

A fragment can't grow, while niches can grow and evolve. The dimension of a fragment doesn't change: it represents the maximum achievable width, and it can't become more significant. A fragment can only get broken into smaller pieces, but it is impossible to increase its dimensions.

In our researches, the term "niche" often emerges.

It is challenging to define the patterns of a niche in research fields. Borrowing some insights from the literature on niches and strategic management (in particular, we refer to the work by Schot & Geels, 2008), we can reflect upon the concept of niches in research. They arise when there is the recognition of a research stream.

Generally speaking, niches arise because scholars focus on some specific issues, a defined and narrow theme. Scholars investigate on a close subject that is linked to a broader topic but is smaller and well defined. When the number of publications, as well as the number of scholars that are interested in this theme, is relevant, then we can have the birth of a niche.

Academic networks support niche development: the broader the relationships among academics are, the more niches are supported in their development. Academicians' expectations contribute to the success of a niche: emerging insights that can be shared among scholars and that provide useful inputs for further research development foster the success of a niche.

We also think that, as suggested by Schot and Geels (2008), the nature of the learning process actively contributes to niche development. In particular, if the result of the research activity is addressed to the creation of changes in cognitive frames and assumptions rather than to data and facts collection, niches are more likely to grow.

The convergence of visions, the happening of learning and experimentation and the building of social networks support the development of a niche (Raven, 2005).

The growth of a niche depends on two issues: the number of publications that cover that particular aspect of the field and the population of scholars that study the topic.

For example, we have examined the distribution of an article whose topic is "green entrepreneur" in the Web of Science database. As a result, we got a total of 676 publications, which shows a growing trend over time. In particular, in 2000, there was a single publication, but in 2019 the total grew by 138. This example shows that niches can grow and they can become wide in terms of the number of publications.

We can say that research in entrepreneurship is made up of niches. Besides a body of research that deals with the broad and general aspect of the theory, issues are then applied to some specific context and, as a consequence, niches arise.

It is not easy to define how many niches can be found in entrepreneurship. We can proceed by adopting two ways of building a taxonomy/classification.

The first way is to explore the groups of scholars; the second method is to examine the emerging insights from the literature.

For what concerns the approach that focuses on scholars, some useful inputs emerge from the work by Gartner et al. (2006): the identification of boundaries as to which scholars pay attention to help to identify labels or niches.[7]

[7] In their work, the authors refer to five main groups: venture capital, corporate entrepreneurship, economist, strategic entrepreneurship and ethnic entrepreneurship.

References

Agarwal, R., & Braguinsky, S. (2015). Industry evolution and entrepreneurship: Steven K lepper's contributions to industrial organization, strategy, technological change, and entrepreneurship. *Strategic Entrepreneurship Journal*, *9*(4), 380–397. Retrieved from http://terpconnect.umd.edu/~rajshree/research/Agarwal and Braguinsky SEJ forthcoming.pdf.

Aldrich, H. E. (2012). The emergence of entrepreneurship as an academic field: A personal essay on institutional entrepreneurship. *Research Policy, 41*(7), 1240–1248.

Aldrich, H. E., & Baker, T. (1997). Blinded by the cites? Has there been progress in entrepreneurship research? In D. L. Sexton & R. W. Smilor (Eds.), *Entrepreneurship 2000* (pp. 377–400). Chicago: Upstart Publishing.

Audretsch, D. (2012). Entrepreneurship research. *Management Decision, 50*(5), 755–764.

Boshoff, A. B., Bennett, H. F., & Owusu, A. A. (1992). Entrepreneurship research: Where are we and where should we be going? *Development Southern Africa*, *9*(1), 47–64. Retrieved from http://www.tandfonline.com/doi/abs/10.1080/03768359208439622.

Bruton, G. D., Ahlstrom, D., & Li, H. (2010). Institutional theory and entrepreneurship: Where are we now and where do we need to move in the future? *Entrepreneurship Theory and Practice, 34*(3), 421–440.

Bruton, G. D., Ahlstrom, D., & Obloj, K. (2008). Entrepreneurship in emerging economies: Where are we today and where should the research go in the future. *Entrepreneurship theory and practice* (Vol. 32, pp. 1–14). Malden, USA: Blackwell Publishing Inc.

Busenitz, L. W., West, G. P., Shepherd, D., Nelson, T., Chandler, G. N., & Zacharakis, A. (2003). Entrepreneurship research in emergence: Past trends and future directions. *Journal of Management, 29*(3), 285–308.

Carlsson, B., Braunerhjelm, P., McKelvey, M., Olofsson, C., Persson, L., & Ylinenpää, H. (2013). The evolving domain of entrepreneurship research. *Small Business Economics, 41*(4), 913–930.

Chandra, Y., & Lozano, S. (2018). Mapping the evolution of entrepreneurship as a field of research (1990–2013): A scientometric analysis. *PLoS ONE*, *13*(1), e0190228.

Cobo, M. J., López-Herrera, A. G., Herrera-Viedma, E., & Herrera, F. (2011). An approach for detecting, quantifying, and visualizing the evolution of a research field: A practical application to the Fuzzy Sets Theory field. *Journal of Informetrics, 5*(1), 146–166.

Coombs, J. E., Sadrieh, F., & Annavarjula, M. (2009). Two decades of international entrepreneurship research: what have we learned where do we go from here? *International Journal of Entrepreneurship, 13,* 23.

Cornelius, B., Landstrom, H., & Persson, O. (2006). Entrepreneurial studies: The dynamic research front of a developing social science. *Entrepreneurship Theory and Practice*, 375–398.

Etzkowitz, H. (2001). The second academic revolution and the rise of entrepreneurial science. *IEEE Technology and Society Magazine, 20*(2), 18–29.

Ferreira, M., Reis, N., & Miranda, R. (2015). Thirty years of entrepreneurship research published in top journals: analysis of citations, co-citations and themes. *Journal of Global Entrepreneurship Research, 5*(1), 1–22.

Gartner, W., Davidsson, P., & Zahra, S. A. (2006). Are you talking to me? The nature of community in entrepreneurship scholarship. *Entrepreneurship Theory and Practice, 30*(3), 321–331.

Gerosa, A., & Tirapani, A. (2013). The culture of entrepreneurship: Creating your own job. *European View, 12*(2), 205–214. Retrieved from http://search.proquest.com/docview/1467021881/.

Harrison, R., & Leitch, C. (1996). Discipline emergence in entrepreneurship: Accumulative fragmentalism or paradigmatic science. *Entrepreneurship: Innovation and Change, 5*(2), 65–83.

Henderson, M., Shurville, S., & Fernstrom, K. (2009). The quantitative crunch: The impact of bibliometric research quality assessment exercises on academic development at small conferences. *Campus-Wide Information Systems, 26*, 149–167.

Hlady-Rispal, M., & Jouison-Laffitte, E. (2014). Qualitative research methods and epistemological frameworks: A review of publication trends in entrepreneurship. *Journal of Small Business Management, 52*(4), 594–614.

Jané, S., Van Esch, C., & Bilimoria, D. (2018). "Why'd you wanna study that?" A process model of the under-legitimation of a research topic. *Academy of Management Learning and Education, 17*(4), 401–424.

Katz, J. A. (2008). Fully mature but not fully legitimate: A different perspective on the state of entrepreneurship education*. *Journal of Small Business Management, 46*(4), 550–566.

Kuhn, T. (1962). *The structure of scientific revolutions*. Chicago: University of Chicago Press.

Kuratko, D. F., & Morris, M. H. (2018). Examining the future trajectory of entrepreneurship. *Journal of Small Business Management, 56*(1), 11–23.

Landstrom, H. (2020). The evolution of entrepreneurship as a scholarly field. *Foundations and Trends in Entrepreneurship, 16*(2), 65–243. https://doi.org/10.1561/0300000083.

Landstrom, H., Harirchi, G., & Astrom, F. (2012). Innovation and entrepreneurship studies: One or two fields of research? In C. Vivas & F. Lucas (Eds.), *Proceedings of the 7th european conference on innovation and entrepreneurship* (Vols. 1 and 2, pp. 420–429).

Link, A. N., Siegel, D. S., & Wright, M. (2015). *The Chicago handbook of university technology transfer and academic entrepreneurship*. Chicago and London: University of Chicago Press.
Lofstrom, M., Bates, T., & Parker, S. C. (2014). Why are some people more likely to become small-businesses owners than others: Entrepreneurship entry and industry-specific barriers. *Journal of Business Venturing, 29*(2), 232–251.
López-Fernández, M. C., Serrano-Bedia, A. M., & Pérez-Pérez, M. (2016). Entrepreneurship and family firm research: A bibliometric analysis of an emerging field. *Journal of Small Business Management, 54*(2), 622–639.
Low, M. B. (2001). The adolescence of entrepreneurship research: Specification of purpose (Business). *Entrepreneurship: Theory and Practice, 25*(4), 17.
Low, M. B., & Macmillan, I. C. (1988). Entrepreneurship: Past research and future challenges. *Journal of Management, 14*(2), 139–161.
Macke, J., Sarate, J. A. R., Domeneghini, J., & Da Silva, K. A. (2018). Where do we go from now? Research framework for social entrepreneurship. *Journal of Cleaner Production, 183,* 677–685.
Matlay, H. (2004). E-entrepreneurship and small e-business development: Towards a comparative research agenda. *Journal of Small Business and Enterprise Development, 11*(3), 408–414.
Mettler, T. (2011). Maturity assessment models: A design science research approach. *International Journal of Society Systems Science, 3*(1/2), 81.
Mitchell, R. K. (2011). Increasing returns and the domain of entrepreneurship research. *Entrepreneurship: Theory and Practice, 35*(4), 615.
Noorden, R. Van. (2013). Open access: The true cost of science publishing. *Nature, 495*(7442), 426.
Noyons, E. C. M., Moed, H. F., & Luwel, M. (1999). Combining mapping and citation analysis for evaluative bibliometric purposes: A bibliometric study. *Journal of the American Society for Information Science, 50,* 115–131.
Onwuegbuzie, A., Johnson, R., & Collins, K. (2011). Assessing legitimation in mixed research: a new framework. *Quality and Quantity, 45*(6), 1253–1271. Retrieved from http://search.proquest.com/docview/898216084/.
Pincock, S. (2013). Publishing: Open to possibilities. *Nature, 495*(7442), 539.
Raven, R. P. J. M. (2005). *Strategic niche management for biomass: A comparative study on the experimental introduction of bioenergy technologies in the Netherlands and Denmark*. Eindhoven: Eindhoven University of Technology.
Reader, D., & Watkins, D. (2006). The social and collaborative nature of entrepreneurship scholarship: A co-citation and perceptual analysis. *Entrepreneurship Theory and Practice, 30*(3), 417–441.
Santini, C. (2011). Chinese immigrants socio-economic enclave in an Italian industrial district: The case of Prato Samuel Rabino Lorenzo Zanni. *World Review, 7*(1), 30–51.

Schildt, H. A., Zahra, S. A., & Sillanpää, A. (2006). Scholarly communities in entrepreneurship research: A co-citation analysis. *Entrepreneurship Theory and Practice, 30*(3), 399–415.

Schot, J., & Geels, F. W. (2008). Strategic niche management and sustainable innovation journeys: Theory, findings, research agenda, and policy. *Technology Analysis & Strategic Management*, *20*(5), 537–554. Retrieved from http://www.tandfonline.com/doi/abs/10.1080/09537320802292651.

Suchman, M. C. (1995). Managing legitimacy—Strategic and institutional approaches. *Academy of Management Review, 20*(3), 571–610.

Tol, R. (2012). Shapley values for assessing research production and impact of schools and scholars. *Scientometrics, 90*(3), 763–780.

van Raan, A. F. J. (2005). Handbook of quantitative science and technology research. In *Chapter Measuring Science* (pp. 19–50). Netherlands: Springer.

Westbrook, L. (1994). Qualitative research methods: A review of major stages, data analysis techniques, and quality controls. *Library & Information Science Research, 16*(3), 241–254.

CHAPTER 2

Good and Entrepreneurship

Abstract This chapter explores the concept of good in entrepreneurship. The debate upon the implication of pursuing good purposes while doing business is vast. This work provides an overview of the main problems that emerge from the literature that investigates how entrepreneurs deal with the achievement of good aims. After having introduced the concept of good in entrepreneurship, the chapter depicts the role that personal values, motivations and beliefs have in shaping entrepreneurial commitment to pursue the good. In this work, we also analyse the role that charisma, personal culture and empathy play in entrepreneurial behaviour. The chapter aims to promote a reflection upon the following questions: What does it mean for an entrepreneur doing the good? What is good for a company? Why some entrepreneurs seem to be particularly willing to pursue the good?

Keywords Good · Entrepreneurship · Personal motivations · Beliefs · Entrepreneur's cultural background · Charisma · Empathy

Introduction

This chapter explores the concept of good in entrepreneurship. The debate upon the implication of pursuing good purposes while doing business is vast. Research in entrepreneurship has underlined the importance

C. Santini, *The Good Entrepreneur*,
https://doi.org/10.1007/978-3-030-59332-2_2

of personal motivation and values in entrepreneurial behaviour. Background literature confirms that ethical and social awareness can strength company vision: they can reinforce the system of relationships with stakeholders; they can help to define corporate image and value proposition; they can support the achievement of competitive advantage.

The approach to "good" has evolved and changed over time: initially, the pursuing of good was a philosophy disconnected to the business culture. The changing of markets, society and business models required top managers and entrepreneurs to include social responsibility within the spectrum of their strategic choices. New needs have emerged from society, and the social landscape reconfiguration has renewed the interest in the pursuit of good.

The Concept of Good in Entrepreneurship

What does it mean for an entrepreneur doing the good? And, as a consequence, what does it mean for an entrepreneur to be good?

Answering this question is extremely challenging.

Generally speaking, we can say that an entrepreneur can do something right if he or she realises something good for the company.

If we change the word "good" with the word "profitable", we overturn the sense of the previous sentence: entrepreneurs do something right for the company when his or her actions bring profits. The provided example introduces the next debate.

Our investigation aimed to maintain a comprehensive perspective; the consideration of *good* can be extended to other stakeholders than the firm. A broad examination about *doing the good* includes a reflection upon society, community or consumers. The pondering of ethical issues in entrepreneurship goes in this direction.

The debate reflects somehow the discussion upon stakeholder value and shareholder value that has animated scholars for a long time.

Shareholders, in general, perceive of primary importance rent generation: in fact, they receive a rent based on the firm's profit (Charreaux & Desbrières, 2001). The concept of value, as we can guess, changes following the characteristics of the firm's strategic perspective: firm's scope is to maximise rents when stakeholders are the primary focus of the company. Therefore, scholars have underlined that creating value for a company can't be reduced to the management of transaction between firms and shareholders (Charreaux & Desbrières, 2001). The academic debate grew, and scholars have highlighted the role of stakeholders in value creation, in corporate governance and strategic choice. Stakeholders put companies under pressure and influence strategic orientation. In some cases, stakeholders can establish a set of rules or regulations that, even if they do not find recognition at an institutional level, can shape firms' behaviour. For what concerns the theme of sustainable development, self-regulatory programmes promoted by stakeholders find a broad diffusion (Perez-Batres, Doh, Miller, & Pisani, 2012).

The perspective of analysis has progressively changed. If initially there was a dualism between shareholder and stakeholder focus, today there is a newer approach that analyses the impact that stakeholders have in the definition of shareholders' set of values, and consequently in shaping the perception of rent and value. Green (1993)—in a paper entitled "Shareholders as Stakeholders: changing metaphors of corporate governance"—outlines that the borders between stakeholders and shareholders are vanishing.

When citing the work by Kenneth Goodpasters, Green (1993) underlines the critical issue in the debate shareholders-stakeholders: "orienting corporate decisions by values that go beyond the long-term maximization of shareholder gain seems essential, yet in some ways illegitimate".

We have dedicated a space to the debate stakeholders-shareholders because we intended to outline similarities in the approach that scholars have had when studying entrepreneurship. We can say that the perception of good, initially, was shaped by a profit-driven approach, and today, it is broader: now it includes a set of values and issues that involve community, environment and other stakeholders.

The Good Entrepreneur, A Matter of Standards

In the literature, we can find many descriptions of good entrepreneurs.

In an article by Casson and Wadeson (2007), we can read that: "Overall, a good entrepreneur, with good judgment, will tend to select good projects, while a bad entrepreneur, with bad judgment, will select bad projects. Of course, given the prohibitive cost of collecting full information, there will always be residual uncertainty; good judgment shortens the odds but does not guarantee success. The new projects promoted by a good entrepreneur will tend to be true opportunities. In contrast, the projects promoted by a bad entrepreneur will be false opportunities—i.e.

projects that appear promising to people who use over-simplified theories and poor information. Investing in false opportunities represents a waste of resources because the opportunities do not belong to the optimal project portfolio. The key to entrepreneurial success is to possess sufficient judgment to recognize true opportunities and screen out false ones" (p. 288).

A good entrepreneur is someone able to recognise excellent opportunities.

The problem is the meaning given to the word *opportunity*: seizing a chance can provide a monetary reward, or it can represent a way to improve the company's ethical orientation. At a personal level, entrepreneurs can evaluate to catch all the opportunities they have to transform their vision into practice.

In any case, according to this definition, to be a good entrepreneur means to be able to catch excellent opportunities.

Nevertheless, for many scholars, a good entrepreneur is someone who owns a set of unique skills (Ray, 1993). The ability to identify new products and opportunities means to be able to see what other people don't recognise, and it is a distinguishing trait of the entrepreneur who is a visionary. Also, persuasive communication skills, together with negotiation skills, are fundamental for spreading entrepreneurs' business idea; they help to share a vision and to attract funds, partners or customers. The ability to achieve effective interpersonal communication—or *people skills*, as defined by Ray (1993)—is crucial for an entrepreneur to succeed. The problem-solving skills are a distinctive trait of a good entrepreneur.

Many scholars have outlined the traits of the entrepreneurs and the related set of distinctive competences. Researchers have highlighted the importance of putting in action some specific behaviours; it remains unsolved the problem of the effectiveness of entrepreneurial behaviour.

Ray (1993) highlights the critical point of the match *being a good entrepreneur* and *owning a set of skills*: "there is no ideal-type personality or marginal set of attributes that guarantee success for a new venture" (p. 354).

Fitting the standards of a good entrepreneur doesn't guarantee that the entrepreneur is a really good one.

This approach introduces further reflection and questions. A big issue is the definition of effectiveness. We could translate "being effective" with "avoiding failures".

It appears that a good entrepreneur is someone who avoids failures and achieves corporate aims. There is another issue that emerges from a reflection on the standard-based approach to "entrepreneurship". If we think about entrepreneurship as alignment to a standard, we facilitate the definition of entrepreneurs, but we also introduce some limits.

The adoption of some models that are undoubtedly successful can create some problems. Our reflection emerges from the insights published by Gerosa and Tirapani (2013) who introduce a phenomenon defined "Silicon Valley Paranoia".

Given the favourable outcomes of the Silicon Valley model, researchers and industries have been attracted by the outstanding example of local high-tech start-ups.

The Silicon Valley model was a source of inspiration for many entrepreneurs but also for many scholars who have pointed to the vibrant community of Californian start-ups for design development paths. In particular, Gerosa and Tirapani (2013) write "We should get rid of the very European idea that we will improve only by copying successful US models, especially that of trying to establish a 'European Silicon Valley'. We think that this 'Silicon Valley paranoia' is what inhibits us from finding a European way for entrepreneurship that better fits our competitive advantage" (p. 212).

The success of entrepreneurs in a defined area can promote stereotype models of entrepreneurship, and the risk is to forget that the success of entrepreneurs in a particular context can be fostered by location. The cultural, social and economic context strongly influences entrepreneurs (Sastre-Castillo, Peris-Ortiz, & Danvila-Del Valle, 2015): this suggests that some "standard models" of entrepreneurs may not work at a global level.

Values and Beliefs

The set of values that belong to an entrepreneur shapes the entrepreneurial idea of good.

In general, the theory supports the idea that entrepreneurial set of values shapes entrepreneurial orientation.

As it emerges in this work, two critical questions for an entrepreneur are: "what does it mean doing the good?" and "what is good?". To answer the above question means to evaluate the entrepreneurial cultural background, set of values and beliefs.

Values are "desirable transituational goals, varying in importance that serve as guiding principles in the life of a person or other social entity" (Schwartz 1992, in Kaesehage et al. 2019).

From this definition, two new issues emerge.

The first is that values are subjective: not all people share the same set of values. We must underline that some authors have highlighted that, given the commonality of human nature, "a set of universal values and standards does exist" (Tsalikis & Seaton, 2007: 230). When a value is shared among the majority, it becomes a norm (Hofstede, 2016). Values can become part of the culture when a collective is involved (Morris & Schindehutte, 2005).

The second issue is that the relevance of value can be different among people.

The intensity of a value (Hofstede, 2016) describes the importance that the value has in an entrepreneur's life. Scholars have tried to develop a taxonomy of values, and in the literature, we can find different classifications that can be employed in the study of human—and entrepreneurial—behaviour.[1] In general, values can be arranged into a hierarchy (Morris & Schindehutte, 2005): some values can be defined as "universal" while others are more specific. Specific values are determined by a set of conditions, such as the political context, institutions or social class. Personal values impact entrepreneurial behaviour since they guide human decisions and actions (Fayolle, Liñán, & Moriano, 2014). Furthermore, every individual establishes a scale of priorities for values. The pyramid of values relates to individual personality traits, attitudes and behaviour (Fayolle et al., 2014).

Therefore, in some cases, it emerges that inputs emerging from the context influence the degree of importance attributed to some issues: the control played by norms or by aggregate cultural values, as well the role of location and local culture, is widely recognised (Fayolle et al., 2014).

[1] In this chapter, we are not going to focus on values taxonomies, but we ought to underline the role covered by the stream of research that has developed between the 1970s and the 1980s that has promoted an active reflection of values as a foundation of human behaviour. A wide overview of the literature can be found in the work (re)published by Hofstede (2016). Yet, we have found extremely interesting the works published by Schwartz (1992) and Schwartz and Bilsky (1990) that are cited also by Morris and Schindehutte (2005).

The literature in this field is endless; in this paragraph, we want to outline an aspect that underlines the potential involvement of an entrepreneur in some specific issues.

Once we have understood the dynamics that explain entrepreneurial behaviour, a question remains open: Why some entrepreneurs are more willing to pursue the good than others?

We know that in some countries, there are conditions that create a breeding ground for an alignment between communities, social or environmental priorities and firms' strategic goals (Fayolle et al., 2014).

Nevertheless, we recommend exploring other problems concerning entrepreneurial awareness further.

Entrepreneurs must be willing to consider needs and motivations that arise from the context (community, market and so forth) and to adopt a stakeholder perspective when defining what is right and valuable for the company.

We have reviewed the literature; the aim was to understand the dynamics that explain the role of personal motivations, values, believes and subjective drivers in shaping the entrepreneurial perception of what is good. The academic literature is extensive, and it touches several aspects including entrepreneurial, ethical motivations and factors (subjective and environmental) that affect moral evaluation and ethics.

Cultural factors affect ethical beliefs and behaviour (Jackson & Artola, 1997; Tsalikis & Seaton, 2007). So, being located in specific area influences also the openness that entrepreneurs might have towards some issues, such as the role of community needs when defining the strategy pursued by the company.

It is in work by Kaesehage et al. (2019) that we find the concept of "distance" to explain the degree of entrepreneurial involvement in proper concerns. The social distance from the object of concern influences the priority given to the problem: "The greater the social distance from the object of concern—i.e. future climate variability—the greater the intellectual doubt, personal sense of helplessness, and uncertainty about the likely success of individual action" (Kaesehage et al., 2019: 1093).

Yet, the intensity of the importance given to the object of concern depends on individual values and beliefs. The perception of the relevance of personal contribution to the well-being of a place or community shapes entrepreneurial priorities' scale. In other words, if people don't consider themselves able to "make the difference" and to contribute to the creation of the well-being of a place, then they would be less motivated to adopt good practices. Background literature supports the presence of a linkage between entrepreneurial orientation and the pursuit of the good; it is also relevant the degree of importance that has within a business contributing to the social, economic and environmental well-being of a community or place (Kaesehage et al., 2019; Thomas & Cross, 2007).

Therefore, in our view, the importance of adopting some socially desirable behaviours shapes the entrepreneurial scale of priorities.

We know about the relevancy of norms; entrepreneurs can be influenced in their conduct by the set of norms and by the desire to align to social standards and external environment. Entrepreneurs, in other words, might feel the pressure to conform to social and political convictions.

The work by Kaesehage et al. (2019) shows the results of some interviews whose focus is sustainability; from this article, we can get a clear idea of the influence of social pressures. The authors write: "Social desirability bias could have influenced the research findings because entrepreneurs might believe it to be socially desirable to wilfully conform to the social, political, and environmental pressures produced by the research (witnessed by the researchers and other entrepreneurs). Entrepreneurs may, for example, respond to interview questions about themselves or their behaviour as a 'positional good' by emphasizing behaviour that is regarded as socially desirable, and thereby underreport behaviour that is perceived as socially inappropriate (see Callegaro, 2008; Densten & Sarros, 2012)" (p. 1105).

The idea of aspiring to what is socially desirable—or to avoid socially inappropriate behaviours—has represented an enlightening insight to us. Academic literature supports the hypothesis that entrepreneurs with their responses seek for social appropriateness.

Yet, the concept of pressure is not new: scholars agree on the role that stakeholders have in shaping the firm's strategy. The relationship between stakeholders' pressure and strategic choices is well described in the paper by Perez-Batres, Doh, Miller, and Pisani (2012). They examine the role of different types of stakeholders in the definition of a corporate social responsibility strategy by firms.

Why Being Good?

The question of *why being good* is not new to research.

Bryant (2009) suggests that this question introduces the following one: who am I?

When answering this question, we need to consider personal issues and the role of the external context. More specifically, entrepreneurs try to be good for many reasons. Entrepreneurs can feel a personal compelling or feel external pressure to adopt specific behaviours; it can happen to have a combination of the two situations.

The literature that explores this issue is endless, and it includes contributions from different fields. What emerges from the multifaceted analysis is the importance covered by the entrepreneur in choosing what relevance give to inputs he gets.

Entrepreneurs have to manage many inputs; they must define a scale of priority and attribute a degree of relevance to the information they perceive.

In other words, the entrepreneur acts like a "filter": he/she collects all the observation that emerges from the external environment and combines them with the personal sphere of motivations and beliefs; then, the decision-making process starts.

This process is well described by Bryant (2009) when he introduces the concept of *self-regulation*.

When talking about self-regulation, we describe a mechanism that disciplines "the selection of ends and means within a framework of moral ideals and norms" (Bryant, 2009: 506).

Self-regulation promotes human thoughts and stimulates a behavioural response; there is a solicitation of individuals for the setting of personal goals and for the definition of paths that steer people towards the achievement of planned objectives. Therefore, self-regulation deals with moral awareness: it determines the strength of ethical awareness among entrepreneurs. There is no doubt that personal issues and cultural background shape entrepreneurial moral consciousness.

Personal Motivations

When carrying this research, we have read many works that explore the role of personal issues and personality traits in entrepreneurship. The importance of entrepreneurial background is pivotal in many publications that explore the theme of awareness concerning social responsibility or openness to social issues.

Entrepreneurs can be more or less receptive to ethical stimuli; it depends on their culture, their background and their sense of belonging to a community. The importance that entrepreneurs give to social issues and the feeling that their decision can improve the well-being of a community shape their approach to social responsibility.

Therefore, the literature makes a further step in the intimate aspects of entrepreneurs as individuals. We think we should make a reflection on mindfulness or emotions because we must underline how complex this issue is. Second, we should reflect on the role covered by different disciplines (such as psychology).

Emotions can influence entrepreneurial mindfulness, and consequently, they influence opportunity recognition (Kelly & Dorian, 2017). Yet, the feeling of compassion (self-compassion and compassion for others) affects entrepreneurs' mindfulness and ethical orientation. The importance of having emotional self-regulation is critical for entrepreneurs who often feel under-pressure; having high levels of emotional regulation means having significant social competences (Kelly & Dorian, 2017).

The approach that focuses on emotional and personal issues of entrepreneurship contributes to filling the gaps in that part of the theory that sees in entrepreneur a rational decision-maker. What emerges from the described approach is an individual with limits from a sociological point of view (Goss, 2005).

Entrepreneurs establish a system of relations that rely on some particular aspects of entrepreneurial charisma and personality. The presence of such a system of relationships can shape the strategic orientation of the firm. Some entrepreneurs can succeed in achieving financial support because they have strong charisma and a dominant personality (Goss, 2005); this means, in other words, that a shadow of subjectivity influences the relationships that involve entrepreneurs.

Words as passion, motivation or emotions are often employed to describe entrepreneurs.

Passion is a dynamic feeling that arises when entrepreneurs are engaged in something "that relates to a meaningful and salient self-identity for them" (Cardon, Wincent, Singh, & Drnovsek, 2009: 516).

Motivations drive entrepreneurs: they decide to undertake something because they are motivated to do it. They can have intrinsic motivations, and they choose to pursue an activity because it is pleasant; sometimes entrepreneurs are engaged in achieving aims, because they represent standards of excellence or because they are a step for a future benefit (Locke & Baum, 2019).

Charisma and Doing Good

Charisma is an *aura* that encourages followers through emotional and ideological contamination (Goss, 2005). Cultures have idealised charisma (Jacquart & Antonakis, 2015), and background literature has explored its relevance in leadership and entrepreneurship.

The definition of the results of charismatic leaders and entrepreneurs is controversial: a hypothetical "evaluation" index can focus on results and performance. In this case, the charisma helps entrepreneurs (or leaders, in general) to promote a valuable operational organisation and to achieve the expected return. Thus, if we think about the role that charisma can play in building relationships, given the ability to generate followers, we adopt a different parameter for evaluating charisma. Jacquart and Antonakis (2015) underline that in the case of a follower-centric perspective, charismatic leadership (or entrepreneurship) is a social construction.

Scholars have explored the role of charisma. Charismatic entrepreneurs and leaders are inspiring, expressive and have the capacity of sharing their intimate vision; they can "touch" people with their message. In their work, Jacquart and Antonakis (2015) depict how the entrepreneurs strategically manage their charismatic skills: entrepreneurs articulate their ideological vision and employ persuasive techniques to deliver a message to followers. Charismatic entrepreneurs "typify the prototypicality that followers seek; they are liked and influence followers because followers identify with them" (Jacquart & Antonakis, 2015: 1054).[2]

The sentiment of correspondence between entrepreneurs and followers is an intriguing issue.

When researching the role of charisma in entrepreneurship, we have found an inspiring input in a publication by Goss (2005). The scholar writes: "the charisma that arises from deference- pride interactions is likely to be inherently fragile, and this often appears the case with businesses developed on this basis: devotion easily turns to disillusionment" (p. 628).

This sense of alignment, correspondence, mutual feeling or identification can turn to disillusion, and the strategy of consensus can quickly fail.

There is no doubt that charisma can be a valuable resource for a company and entrepreneurs. Still, they have to be able to build a strategy

[2] In this paper, Jacquart & Antonakis (2015), refer to leaders, but the insights reported in the background section can be generalized and referred to entrepreneurs.

that exploits their charismatic skills so to ensure the sustainability of the strategy itself.

Some people may object to recognise the strategic importance of charisma. Yet from the literature, it emerges the decisive role that charisma has in fundraising (Yusuf, 2011); this is only one of the many areas of interest of charisma. Furthermore, charisma can help entrepreneurs to build a stable relationship with other stakeholders.

The critical issue, as it emerges from (Goss, 2005), is to avoid the danger of turning devotion to disillusion. Thus, when entrepreneurs show to care about ethical issues or about issues that are connected to people's health or welfare, it is easier to build relationships with followers that are going to be long-lasting over time.

Therefore, charismatic entrepreneurs can promote a sensitisation towards the aims of their vision.

In the literature about green entrepreneurship, the association between charisma and entrepreneurs often emerges. Visionary entrepreneurs, also defined as "sea-change", are charismatic persons that, in the cases explored by (Walley, Taylor, & Greig, 2010), promote a vision of their business that encompasses sustainable principles.[3]

When the charisma is based upon the ability of an entrepreneur to embrace principles and values that stand at the basis of the social welfare or that encounter the common sense of good, here stand the premises for the establishment of a long-term relationship with followers.

An entrepreneur whose charisma derives from a personal orientation towards what is considered ethical can reduce the risk of failure, connected to followers' disillusion.

Personal Culture and Doing Good

There is no doubt that there is a link between entrepreneurship and culture. In 2010, Naughton and Cornwall published an article entitled "Culture as the Basis of The Good Entrepreneur" that explores the linkages between culture, entrepreneurship and good. The perception of what is right is influenced by culture.

[3] In their work, the authors also refer to the "classic" example of Anita Roddick of Body Shop fame, who is energetic, visionary and charismatic.

Among the various definitions of culture, we refer to the one by Naughton and Cornwall (2009) who write: "culture is a common way of life" (p. 11).

This immediate definition quickly highlights the inspiring sharing principle of culture formation; culture permeates all the aspects of life, so it is a way of life.

Therefore, culture is determined by a set of issues, and family and education are two of its pillars. Even religion can actively shape culture.

Many researchers have demonstrated how religion can inspire entrepreneurial behaviour: it is the case of Muslim entrepreneurs in India or Malaysia. In both instances, entrepreneurs in the light of their religious orientation have developed a sense of responsibility towards the whole community (Osella & Osella, 2009). Several scholars have explored the relationship between religion and entrepreneurship. It emerges that no matter what is the faith, but entrepreneurs who are inspired by religious motives embrace similar patterns (Dana, 2009) and in general develop an inner sensitivity for the community and its needs. As well as religion, a strong personal motivation that derives from a solid educational background can foster openness to the pursuit of good.

Empathy and Philanthropy

We have highlighted the importance of personal motives in pursuing the good. We know that feelings play a central role in the development of a doing-well-by-doing-good strategy. We also know that entrepreneurs might feel the urgency of doing something right. We can find entrepreneurs who dedicate time and money to some good causes. Some entrepreneurs personify the essence of patronage; in some cases, philanthropic entrepreneurs support local communities, or they offer their financial aid for helping people that are encountering difficulties in a specific period. In other cases, we find entrepreneurs who create an enterprise whose aim is to fulfil social needs: it is the case, among the others, of non-profit businesses.

What we want to outline is that entrepreneurs can find different ways to put in practice their willingness to help people; social context, location and personal motivations can play an essential role in defining how to help people.

In our view, location nurtures a philanthropic aptitude.

In some countries, some conditions promote corporate philanthropy; the presence of a favourable context—due to a mix of legal, political-economic and cultural factor—can improve philanthropy (Gautier & Pache, 2015).

Some countries, such as the USA or UK, have a long tradition with philanthropy; this is because donators can benefit from a set of norms and legal conditions that ease and favour financial support. If we take a virtual tour of the *Chronicle of Philanthropy*, we can have a clear idea of the measures that support a philanthropic approach in the USA, from an organisational, legal and financial point of view. In 2019, in the USA, giving reached 400 billion USD and new needs and trends emerged.

This book wants to explore the relationship between entrepreneurs and the pursuit of the good; in the light of this, we want to point out a few issues that are reshaping the concept of giving and donating. We take as a benchmark the report published by the Jhonson Center[4] that highlights the emerging transformation in the sector of giving. As it emerges from the document, we are witnesses of a "blurriness of sector boundaries"; it becomes difficult to distinguish between for-profit and non-profit or business and philanthropic sectors.

We cite a part of the report that depicts the dynamics of giving: "More non-profits are looking for profitable revenue streams and borrowing business jargon and tactics. More donors are talking about their giving and grantmaking as "social investing," and are conducting "due diligence" on these investments. On the corporate side, Milton Friedman is rolling in his grave as "corporate social responsibility" is becoming a requirement for businesses of all sorts. Even Super Bowl ads are touting each company's charitable or environmental commitments as much as the quality of their products (Schultz, 2018). If you aren't a double- or triple-bottom-line company, you can't compete anymore. (…) In short, philanthropy is increasingly adopting business means, while business is increasingly pursuing philanthropic ends" (p. 5).

Philanthropic entrepreneurs are turning into social entrepreneurs. The introduction of due diligence in donation suggests us a further question: Why the need for a set of standards emerges? Why people need due diligence in donations? We have found illuminating one consideration that appears from the article by Frumkin (2003) who writes: "Many

[4] The report is available at the following website: https://johnsoncenter.org/11-trends-for-2019/.

donors, particularly those who have made money in business, find the lack of standards and benchmarks in the world of philanthropy particularly troubling" (p. 13).

Entrepreneurs are shaped by their experience in business that stimulates their approach to donations: personal traits, that are strictly related to skills, competences and way of organising roles and duties, unavoidably shape the way entrepreneurs behave and conceive the management of donations. The emerging insights from Frumkin (2003) provide a useful perspective for "reading" the report published by the Jhonson Center.

Therefore, as we already have underlined, some conditions stimulate an orientation towards donation and philanthropy. In addition to the set of favourable circumstances that emerge from location, companies with a higher net income tend to give more (Gautier & Pache, 2015).

Then, there are personal motivations that drive entrepreneurs and managers to adopt altruistic behaviour. The imperative of doing something right and giving space to ethical motives is particularly high when entrepreneurs don't get much exposure from their philanthropic decisions. Yet, self-identification of entrepreneurs as philanthropists promotes a humane approach (Gautier & Pache, 2015). As we can observe, again, a mix of factors concurs in shaping the orientation towards giving and donating. It is incredibly challenging to define how altruistic and philanthropic attitude shapes entrepreneurial behaviour. We can say that the input of doing something good for others can turn into giving financial support and that there is a set of condition that facilitates altruistic behaviours.

Doing Well and Good

The combination of doing well and good (DWDGG) is an issue that is quite popular among scholars. Researchers' attention has focused on the following questions: How can we combine doing well and good? The problems explored vary from the struggle between the necessity to gain profits and the need to pursue something good, to the role of CSR in entrepreneurial decisions.

The debate about doing well and doing good is "one of the dominant themes of business ethics" (Nguyen & Cragg, 2012: 53).

Scholars have explored the strategic importance of ethical issues that can be a way for achieving competitive advantage (Porter & Kramer, 2006).

Yet some authors have been extremely sceptical when analysing the motto "Doing Well by Doing Good" (DWDG).

Karnani (2011) writes: "while appealing DWDG is also a fundamentally wrong proposition" (p. 70). The motivations why the author expresses critiques to the DWDG preposition are rooted in the theoretical background. In particular, market efficiency should ensure the alignment between private profits and public interests.

This insight finds further explanation in what Karnani (2011) writes: "In an efficient market, every profitable firm is doing good. Customers who buy from the company do so voluntarily and must derive value greater than the price paid; this is the consumer surplus, which contributes to social welfare. Companies provide employment and pay taxes—all good for society. However, this is trivializing the notion of "doing good"; all this social value is a by-product of firms maximizing profits. For the CSR proposition to have any real substance, the firm has to produce more social value than a normal profit-maximizing firm; there has to be a divergence, a trade-off between profit-maximizing strategies and social welfare" (p. 71).

The system of causal nexus outlined by Karnani (2011) proposes a further reflection on the effectiveness of some theoretical background issues. If everything went smoothly, probably, there would not have been a debate on the importance of pursuing the good. What is extremely interesting to us is the role that scholar's approach has in shaping theoretical contributions. The cited article has, at its foundation, the power of the regulatory structure of the market. The debate vigorously emerges in a paper published in the same journal, The California Management Review, the same year. The article is entitled "*The grand misapprehension. A response to Doing Well by Doing Good: The Grand Illusion*" and it is a critical essay by Rivoli and Waddock (2011).

The authors underline that the equation that correlates market efficiency to profitable firms that seek for good is not so immediate. According to Rivoli and Waddock (2011): "good goes beyond economics to encompass well-being, health, equity, and sustainability, to name a few "goods." That is, the societal perspective argues that things beyond (but including) economics are essential goods for a wide variety of stakeholders, many of whom contribute to the wealth creation potential of firms (e.g., employees, customers, suppliers, and communities—in addition to investors)" (p. 114). Reading the two article is an exciting experience since it highlights the importance of this debate and the theoretical questions and approaches that emerge when dealing with this issue.

To give an idea about the relevance of the topic "doing well and doing good", we have performed a basic search on WOS database to highlight in how many journal articles the DWDG sentence appears in the title.

The first articles appear in 2009, and out of the 53 records, 24 belong to the category "business". The majority of the cited articles focuses on corporate social responsibility. The problem of DWDG is often related to corporate social responsibility; in general, what emerges from a very rough analysis is the well-known contraposition between profits and ethical or social issues. In our opinion, the critical question for scholars is to do something right while doing well or in other words, to pursue noble goals while making money.

In our research, we have had the chance to read an interesting article by Margolis (2008) published on the Harvard Business Review. In this article, we can understand that among the various forms of social responsibility, "cash contributions to charities have shown a stronger correlation with success than have socially responsible corporate policies or community projects" (p. 18).

Pursuing the good by doing well is not so easy: it requires the development of a mindset, the creation of corporate culture and the implementation of ethical issues in corporate management. If we analyse the quotation from Margolis (2008) with this perspective, we can fully understand the proposed message. We can say that it is more comfortable doing well and doing good than doing well by doing good.

Entrepreneurs as Change Agents

Many scholars see entrepreneurs as change agents. This assumption arises from the direct observation of entrepreneurs in action or from an analysis of the consequences of entrepreneurial activities.

Entrepreneurs hold a responsibility, given their power of changing the social or economic reality they experience. They can trigger a good or an adverse change: everything depends on their behaviour and the aims they pursue.

Why entrepreneurs become changing agents?

Under what conditions they can make the difference and change a scenario?

A good starting point for answering these questions is a consideration of the characteristics of entrepreneurs as leaders. There is no doubt that entrepreneurs should have certain credibility to gain followers. In an article on social entrepreneurship, Waddock and Post (1991) describe the dynamics of change—more precisely "catalytic change"—undertaken by social entrepreneurs. Entrepreneurs have some features that make it possible to engage with others "in such a way that leaders and followers raise one another to higher levels of motivation and morality" (p. 395).

The ability to create a connection with other people, based on personal credibility and commitment, together with a strong motivation to pursue collective purpose, is a crucial asset for managing the innate complexity of some social problems. The creation of a relationship, leader-follower, is vital for facing the multiple complexity—or multiplicity—of social issues: this is because entrepreneurs who are engaged with everyday purposes or social issues must adopt a *step-by-step* strategy, since "The initiatives generated by these entrepreneurs are necessarily viewed as the first of one of many steps needed to actually resolve the problem" (Waddock & Post, 1991: 395).

In the light of the above consideration, we can say that entrepreneurs can act as change agents if they can establish relationships with other people who are willing to follow them. The more complex the problem is, the stronger this relationship built on credibility and shared commitment should be.

There is another interesting aspect that emerges, and it deals with the capacity of social entrepreneurs to vehicle different types of resources to a social aim.[5] In some cases, entrepreneurs combine companies whose primary objective is to not social, to participate to some social purposes; in other words, they indirectly share their visions with other companies and make them part of a social change. Under this perspective, entrepreneurs can instil in other business partners the desire to make the difference.

In this paragraph, we have explored the "social side" of entrepreneurs; thus, entrepreneurs can make change happen even if they are not social

[5] "The social entrepreneurs, therefore, brought together resources from numerous organizations whose primary goals are indirectly or in the long term affected. (...) This intermingling of different goals complicates an already complex situation" (Waddock & Post, 1991: 395–396).

entrepreneurs. The linkage between a switch and entrepreneurship overwhelmingly explodes when we think about social entrepreneurship, and it helps us to add other pieces to the puzzle.

Entrepreneurs can become changing innovators because of the innovativeness of their ideas, products, businesses or approaches. Some volcanic entrepreneurs have literately revolutionised an industry, or a community, by introducing innovative technologies, for example. The academic literature that deals with the "disruptive power" of entrepreneurs is endless. We have performed a basic search on the specialised press, and we have checked some publications such as Forbes.

There is an abundance of articles that depict successful stories of entrepreneurs that have changed the business; these entrepreneurs, in some cases, have created opportunities for increasing stakeholders or communities' well-being. Yet, there is a linkage between entrepreneurial success and the chance to make a change: successful entrepreneurs might reinvest their profit locally. Under this perspective, successful entrepreneurs can shape the local environment and create the condition for change happening.

References

Bryant, P. (2009). Self-regulation and moral awareness among entrepreneurs. *Journal of Business Venturing, 24*(5), 505–518.

Callegaro, M. (2008). Encyclopedia of Survey Research Methods. SAGE Research Methods. *Social Desirability*. Retrieved from https://srmo.sagepub.com/view/encyclopedia-of-survey-research-methods/n537.xml.

Cardon, M., Wincent, J., Singh, J., & Drnovsek, M. (2009). The nature and experience of entrepreneurial passion. *Academy of Management Review, 34*(3), 511–532. Retrieved from http://search.proquest.com/docview/37167064/.

Casson, M., & Wadeson, N. (2007). The discovery of opportunities: Extending the economic theory of the entrepreneur. *Small Business Economics, 28*(4), 285–300.

Charreaux, G., & Desbrières, P. (2001). Corporate governance: Stakeholder value versus shareholder value. *Journal of Management and Governance, 5*(2), 107–128.

Dana, L. P. (2009). Religion as an explanatory variable for entrepreneurship. *The International Journal of Entrepreneurship and Innovation, 10*(2), 87–99.

Densten, I. L., & Sarros, J. C. (2012). The impact of organizational culture and social desirability on Australian CEO leadership. *Leadership & Organization Development Journal, 33*(4), 342–368.

Fayolle, A., Liñán, F., & Moriano, J. (2014). Beyond entrepreneurial intentions: Values and motivations in entrepreneurship. *International Entrepreneurship and Management Journal, 10*(4), 679–689.

Frumkin, P. (2003). Inside venture philanthropy. *Society, 40*(4), 7–15.

Gautier, A., & Pache, A.-C. (2015). Research on corporate philanthropy: A review and assessment. *Journal of Business Ethics, 126*(3), 343–369.

Gerosa, A., & Tirapani, A. (2013). The culture of entrepreneurship: creating your own job. *European View, 12*(2), 205–214. Retrieved from http://search.proquest.com/docview/1467021881/.

Goss, D. (2005). Entrepreneurship and 'the social': Towards a deference-emotion theory. *Human Relations, 58*(5), 617–636.

Green, R. M. (1993). Shareholders as stakeholders: Changing metaphors of corporate governance. (Symposium: New Directions in Corporate Law). *Washington and Lee Law Review, 50*(4), 1421.

Hofstede, G. (2016). Culture's consequences: Comparing values, behaviors, institutions, and organizations across nations (2nd ed.). *Collegiate Aviation Review, 34*(2), 108–109. Retrieved from http://search.proquest.com/docview/1841323332/.

Jackson, T., & Artola, M. (1997). Ethical beliefs and management behaviour: A cross-cultural comparison. *Journal of Business Ethics, 16*(11), 1163–1173.

Jacquart, P., & Antonakis, J. (2015). When does charisma matter for top-level leaders? effect of attributional ambiguity. *Academy of Management Journal, 58*(4), 1051. retrieved from http://search.proquest.com/docview/1709998736/.

Kaesehage, K., Leyshon, M., Ferns, G., & Leyshon, C. (2019). Seriously personal: The reasons that motivate entrepreneurs to address climate change. *Journal of Business Ethics, 157*(4), 1091–1109. https://doi.org/10.1007/s10551-017-3624-1.

Karnani, A. (2011). "Doing well by doing good": The grand illusion. *California Management Review, 53*(2), 69–86. Retrieved from http://search.proquest.com/docview/865526128/.

Kelly, L., & Dorian, M. (2017). Doing well and good: An exploration of the role of mindfulness in the entrepreneurial opportunity recognition and evaluation process. *New England Journal of Entrepreneurship, 20*(2), 26–36.

Locke, E. A., & Baum, J. R. (2019). Passion and Entrepreneurship. In *Passion for work*. Oxford: Oxford University Press.

Margolis, J. (2008). Do well by doing good? Don't count on it. *Harvard Business Review, 86*(1), 19–20. Retrieved from http://search.proquest.com/docview/227837475/.

Morris, M., & Schindehutte, M. (2005). Entrepreneurial values and the ethnic enterprise: An examination of six subcultures. *Journal of Small Business Management, 43*(4), 453–479.

Naughton, M., & Cornwall, J. (2009). Culture as the basis of the good entrepreneur. *Journal of Religion and Business Ethics, 1*(1). Retrieved from http://search.proquest.com/docview/1798283612/.

Nguyen, A., & Cragg, W. (2012). Interorganizational favour exchange and the relationship between doing well and doing good. *Journal of Business Ethics, 105*(1), 53–68.

Osella, F., & Osella, C. (2009). Muslim entrepreneurs in public life between India and the Gulf: Making good and doing good. *Journal of the Royal Anthropological Institute, 15*(15), S202–S221.

Perez-Batres, L., Doh, J., Miller, V., & Pisani, M. (2012). Stakeholder pressures as determinants of CSR strategic choice: Why do firms choose symbolic versus substantive self-regulatory codes of conduct? *Journal of Business Ethics, 110*(2), 157–172. Retrieved from http://search.proquest.com/docview/1069314302/.

Porter, M. E., & Kramer, M. R. (2006). Strategy and society: The link between competitive advantage and corporate social responsibility. *Harvard Business Review, 84*(12), 78.

Ray, D. (1993). Understanding the entrepreneur—Entrepreneurial attributes, experience and skills. *Entrepreneurship and Regional Development, 5*(4), 345. Retrieved from http://search.proquest.com/docview/38446602/.

Rivoli, P., & Waddock, S. (2011). The grand misapprehension (a response to' "doing well by doing good": The grand illusion') (Critical essay). *California Management Review, 53*(2), 112–116.

Sastre-Castillo, M. A., Peris-Ortiz, M., & Danvila-Del Valle, I. (2015). What is different about the profile of the social entrepreneur? *Nonprofit Management and Leadership, 25*(4), 349–369.

Schwartz, S. H. (1992). Universals in the content and structure of values: Theoretical advances and empirical tests in 20 countries. In M. Zanna (Ed.), *Advances in experimental social psychology* (pp. 1–65). Orlando: Academic Press.

Schwartz, S. H., & Bilsky, W. (1990). Toward a theory of the universal content and structure of values: Extensions and cross-cultural replications. *Journal of Personality and Social Psychology, 58*(5), 878.

Thomas, D. F., & Cross, J. E. (2007). Organizations as place builders. *Journal of Behavioral and Applied Management, 9*(1), 33.

Tsalikis, J., & Seaton, B. (2007). The international business ethics index: European union. *Journal of Business Ethics, 75*(3), 229–238.

Waddock, S. A., & Post, J. E. (1991). Social entrepreneurs and catalytic change. *Public Administration Review, 51*(5), 401.

Walley, L., Taylor, D., & Greig, K. (2010). Beyond the visionary champion. *Making Ecopreneurs: Developing ....* Retrieved from https://books.google.

com/books?hl=en&lr=&id=AIRILhGp3yUC&oi=fnd&pg=PA59&dq=ecopreneurship&ots=bGnJ0Ix7El&sig=I9M_7A_QSjcD8lhOF0YD-yTaD1c.

Yusuf, J.-E. (2011). The entrepreneur-investor charismatic relationship: A dramaturgical approach. *Journal of Enterprising Culture, 19*(04), 373–396.

CHAPTER 3

Social Entrepreneurship

Abstract This work examines the issue of social entrepreneurship. The chapter aims to explore the determinants of social entrepreneurship and the dynamics of this research field. The versatility of the term has boosted its diffusion and facilitated its employment for describing many different enterprises and entrepreneurs. After having defined social entrepreneurship, the chapter highlights the traits of this type of entrepreneur. A section is dedicated to the role the entrepreneurs have in the facing of global health challenges and natural disasters.

Keywords Social entrepreneurship · Natural disaster · Global health challenges

Introduction

The research field of entrepreneurship is endless. The birth of research niches has provoked a debate. With regard to the issue of good pursuing, we can see that over time, new types of entrepreneurs have emerged. Background literature shows that entrepreneurs are progressively focusing their attention on issues different from making profits. Even the dualism "profit – values" that has attracted scholars' interest for such a long time seems to be on its way to find a happy end. In this chapter, we will make a further step to understand who is a good entrepreneur. We will start from

C. Santini, *The Good Entrepreneur*,
https://doi.org/10.1007/978-3-030-59332-2_3

social entrepreneurs: they represent a relevant share of the population of *good entrepreneurs*, from an academic point of view. We aim to understand what are the traits of social entrepreneurship, why it is growing, and what motivates its growth.

Categories of Good Entrepreneurs

We have seen that entrepreneurs distinguish themselves from a set of characteristics; they behave in a certain way, by showing risk-taking proclivity or being able to seize opportunities.

We have also seen that the idea that limits the pursuit of good to profit achievement is limited.

Therefore, we have seen that the influence of personal characteristics and the need to answer to some specific requirements that emerge from the market or society leads entrepreneurs to follow new paths or to introduce new issues in their mindset.

A new type of entrepreneurs has emerged over time.

In this chapter, we will focus on some definitions of entrepreneurs that academicians widely use. All the different types of entrepreneurs share the care for issues that are valuable for stakeholders or communities. Under this perspective, we define them *good entrepreneurs,* since one of their aims—primary or secondary—is to pursue the common good.

A proliferation of categories and types of entrepreneurs emerge; we refer in our approach to what emerges from our study on research niches in entrepreneurship: each group of entrepreneurs in this chapter has a corresponding research niche. In other words, we are considering terms that show a relevant degree of academic consideration and that are recognised by scholars or associations. All the typologies of entrepreneurs we are considering have their definitions and have a defined research stream.

Research shows that a taxonomy of good entrepreneurs can be achieved by focusing on the main scope of their activities. Yet good entrepreneurs can be inspired by social, ethical or environmental motives. Therefore, when we talk about good entrepreneurs, we are talking about: social entrepreneurs; green entrepreneurs; sustainable entrepreneurs (or sustainopreneur); ecopreneurs; enviropreneurs.

Research is relatively new with referral to some specific categories that have found a recent development; in other cases, as we will see later in this book, research has a long history.

Social Entrepreneurship

Social entrepreneurship became one of the most vivid research fields in the area of entrepreneurship. The first to employ the term "social entrepreneur" was Joseph Banks in 1972; the author explained that society needed some managerial skills to solve some social problems (Ebrashi, 2013).

The roots of this "niche" date back to the 1980s, with the work of Bill Drayton, who founded Ashoka, an association that promotes social entrepreneurship.

Drayton had the merit to diffuse the term "social entrepreneur". A marked focus on social mission characterises the social entrepreneur. Social value in social entrepreneurship is, as Ebrashi (2013) suggests, "the explicit and central driving force" (p. 189); social entrepreneurs show a strong commitment to producing social impact and social change.

The topic of social entrepreneurship has attracted fascinated universities and has shaped not only their research strategies but also their educational offerings.

Universities have developed educational and research programmes in social entrepreneurship: among the others, we cite the educational programmes run by the University of Pennsylvania, Oxford University, Duke, Yale, Stanford, University of California-Berkeley, Northwestern University, Harvard, University of Michigan, Cornell University, Babson College, the University of Colorado at Boulder, Boston College, New York University, Carnegie Mellon University, Indiana University Bloomington, Georgetown, Pepperdine and so forth.

This long list—still uncomplete and focusing on a limited geographical area—gives an idea of the relevance of social entrepreneurship from an educational point of view.

Scholars have investigated the motivations and the dynamics of education in social entrepreneurship; among the various articles, we think that the work by Mirabella and Young (2012) provides insights for understanding the motivations behind the academic interest in social entrepreneurship educational programmes. First, over the years, we register a progressive establishment of business management solutions to public problems; this fully motivates the importance given by business schools to social entrepreneurship. The authors suggest that educational programmes go in the direction of providing more comprehensive curricula that include a focus on non-profit skills also in business schools, not only in public administration and policy curricula.

We have a preliminary idea of the relevance of the "niche" of social entrepreneurship.

We have carried out a preliminary review of the main articles that have mapped or have analysed the significant contributions in the field. There is an article recently published by Ferreira, Fernandes, and Kraus (2019) that explores research in entrepreneurship; the authors outline the importance of developing a social entrepreneurship theory, since "Only by doing this can entrepreneurial processes occurring in non-governmental organizations be explained. Furthermore, these cases of entrepreneurship are driven by motivations different from profit-seeking companies" (p. 197).

From the literature (Persaud, Bayon, & Cartmell, 2018), in general, it emerges that even if the topic attracts many scholars and the number of publications boomed, especially after 2010, research still needs to be further developed. The majority of the studies are, according to some authors (Persaud et al., 2018), conceptual and descriptive and case-based. Research is, furthermore, geographically concentrated in North America and the UK. There is no doubt that this is an evolving and promising field of study. Yet, in the next paragraphs, we will provide insights for a better understanding of the dynamics that explain social entrepreneurship.

Growth and Drivers

Research on social entrepreneurship has registered an increase, since its early beginnings. We will see in the next chapters the evolution of this niche when observing the number of publications in the field. Several factors have contributed to the growth of this research niche.

The term social entrepreneurship has found a vast diffusion for identifying different concepts or situations. It was primarily used to identify a specific firm ownership structure (e.g. cooperatives), fundraising ventures in the non-profit context or business ventures with social purposes (Hockerts, 2006). The versatility of the term has boosted its diffusion and facilitated its employment for describing many different enterprises and entrepreneurs.

There is no doubt that when scholars find a consensus among institutions and supporters, it is easier to register a growth in terms of research outputs.

Foundations have risen to support social entrepreneurs and related academic research; the World Economic Forum itself has focused his attention on this issue. The activity of some foundations has nurtured a culture of social entrepreneurship: the story of the Schwab Foundation reveals the pivotal role that this organisation has in the development of a changing culture and the support of social entrepreneurs' initiatives.[1] Yet, the number of foundations that support social entrepreneurship is vast, and some of them operate at a global level and others have a local scope.

Organizations with a specific focus on social entrepreneurship, started to emerge in the early 1980s: Ashoka was founded in 1981, the Skoll Foundation in 1999, the Schwab Foundation in 1998 and later we find UnLtd (2002) and the Young Foundation (2006), just to cite few examples.

We can say that since the late 1970s-early 1980s a process of awareness started, involving organisations as well as institutions: governments were attracted by the possibility of bettering the management of social issues through welfare (Ebrashi, 2013).

Finally, in the process of global recognition of social entrepreneurship, the Nobel Prize given to Muhammad Yunus played a pivotal role (Kickul, Terjesen, Bacq, & Griffiths, 2012).

The issue of social entrepreneurship became popular; we can foresee the reasons behind this popularity from what we have previously described. Roger and Osberg (2007) provide a clear description of the motives that make social entrepreneurship a popular research niche destined to grow. The authors explain that some motivations are fundamental, and they are inherent to the appealing of these kinds of entrepreneurs and their stories. The idea of being responsible for the improvement of so many lives is extremely attracting: "Social entrepreneurship signals the imperative to drive social change, and it is that potential payoff, with its lasting, transformational benefit to society, that sets the field and its practitioners apart" (p. 30).

[1] We suggest to take a look at the Schwab Foundation web page https://www.schwabfound.org/. Many resources and reports can be downloaded; they introduce to the topic of social entrepreneur, describe their activities and also provide a description of the impact of their activity. The website provides many inputs for understanding why social entrepreneurs are changing agents.

The authors underline a critical aspect of social entrepreneurship: "Although the potential benefits offered by social entrepreneurship are clear to many of those promoting and funding these activities, the actual definition of what social entrepreneurs do to produce this order of magnitude return is less clear. We would argue that the definition of social entrepreneurship today is anything but clear. As a result, social entrepreneurship has become so inclusive that it now has a large tent into which all manners of socially beneficial activities fit. In some respects, this inclusiveness could be a good thing. If plenty of resources are pouring into the social sector, and if many causes that otherwise would not get sufficient funding now get support because they are regarded as social entrepreneurship, then it may be fine to have a loose definition" (p. 30).

The "secret" of the appeal of social entrepreneurship is that it holds a promise: there is still much to do for understanding this phenomenon, but there is no doubt that it is intriguing.

Research in social entrepreneurship has followed the same dynamics that we have observed when dealing with the development of research in entrepreneurship. We refer to that phenomenon that correlates the academic interest to the industry interest. Mair, Robinson, and Hockerts (2006) write: "we observe that the rise of scholarly interest in social entrepreneurship goes hand in hand with an increasing interest in the phenomenon among elites. Over the last few years, many successful business entrepreneurs have dedicated substantial resources to supporting social entrepreneurship" (p. 1).

Generally speaking, we can say that research in social entrepreneurship grew because it finds a consensus among various stakeholders, and in particular, institutions, industry and society. The active role of institutions and foundations has created awareness towards this issue through some educational programmes or financial support.

From our research, another factor that has contributed to the growth of social entrepreneurship emerges: today the society is in search of a renewed sense of community. We are assisting to a social transformation, and society is becoming more fluid and individualised (Leadbeater, 1997). The ongoing globalisation and the problems arising with migrations suggest that communities built on hierarchical and conservative principles might not work; social entrepreneurs can be a cornerstone for establishing a "modern sense of community" (Leadbeater, 1997: 16). Therefore, society and the ongoing social transformation give space to social entrepreneurship.

The Characteristics

Much research has focused on providing cases and examples of social entrepreneurs, and this is the reason why Mair et al. (2006) talk about phenomenon-driven research.

The first point is to define social entrepreneurship. As it can be guessed, it is hard to find a unique and commonly employed definition, given the broad range of meanings that this concept gains among researchers.[2] Swanson and Di Zhang (2010) underline that, despite the absence of a common agreement on a definition for social entrepreneurship among scholars, there is a consensus on its goals.

The approach adopted by Hockerts (2006) is intriguing because he classifies the attempts to define social entrepreneurs into two main categories according to the employed perspective. The first is the individual perspective, and the second is an organisational perspective. The individual view poses at the centre of the analysis the personal motivations and commitment that inspire social entrepreneurs. The organisational perspective classifies social enterprises (and social entrepreneurs' behaviour) into three categories: the first one is the case of companies and entrepreneurs who commercialise non-profit organisations. In other words, social entrepreneurs who belong to this category create profits for non-profit companies. The second case is the so-called efficient non-profit management, that is, bringing marketing and business skills in the non-profit sector. The second approach focuses on social purpose business ventures; the competitive proposition of this kind of enterprises is the opportunity that arises from social innovation. Social entrepreneurs realise profits through social change and create a market space where they can compete.

What distinguishes social entrepreneurship from entrepreneurship is—as Roger and Osberg (2007) say—the primacy of social benefit: social entrepreneurs combine the typical traits of entrepreneurs, such as innovativeness or risk-taking attitude, to a focus on social benefit. The work by Roger and Osberg (2007) provides many examples of social

[2] There are many works that provide a detailed overview of definitions and meanings for social entrepreneurship and social enterprise. Among them, we found the work by Marti (2004) extremely useful. We will use this work as a reference for organizing information about social entrepreneurship.

entrepreneurs, and it highlights three components that help to identify social entrepreneurship.

"We define social entrepreneurship as having the following three components: (1) identifying a stable but inherently unjust equilibrium that causes the exclusion, marginalization, or suffering of a segment of humanity that lacks the financial means or political clout to achieve any transformative benefit on its own; (2) identifying an opportunity in this unjust equilibrium, developing a social value proposition, and bringing to bear inspiration, creativity, direct action, courage, and fortitude, thereby challenging the stable state's hegemony; and (3) forging a new, stable equilibrium that releases trapped potential or alleviates the suffering of the targeted group, and through imitation and the creation of a stable ecosystem around the new equilibrium ensuring a better future for the targeted group and even society at large" (p. 35).

Social entrepreneurship represents a mean of creating initiatives and innovative solutions whose ultimate aim is to support a sustainable and social transformation (Alvord, Brown, & Letts, 2004). For other scholars, it is an approach that brings innovative and sustainable solutions to solve social market failure by seizing opportunities (Mair et al., 2006; Marti, 2004). Others highlight the multidimensional construct of social entrepreneurship that brings together a personal entrepreneurial vision, characteristics and behaviours addressed to the achievement of a social mission (Sullivan Mort, Weerawardena, & Carnegie, 2003).

From a review of the scholars' contributions, we can see that the central concepts associated with social entrepreneurship are not only innovativeness, value creation, change and transformation but also problem-solving. The literature recognises social entrepreneurs the ability to solve problems more effectively than the government due to their capacity of tailoring their efforts to different communities and markets (Dees, 2007). Therefore, social entrepreneurs are problem solvers, not only because they contribute to solving some challenges that are affecting a community or a particular area, but also because they can assist the government.

In general, we can say that a social entrepreneur gives particular emphasis to some selected issues during strategic planning. In other words, social entrepreneurs show sensitivity towards some elements that put decision-making under pressure. Pressures can be both bottom-up or top-down: we refer to bottom-up drivers if the pressure comes from stakeholders that are ideally located one or more steps under the entrepreneur in a hypothetical positioning scale. Institutions, for example, execute a top-down pressure, since they are on the upper level of a hierarchical pyramid. In any case, drivers foster entrepreneurs' motivations and shape their decision.

Social entrepreneurs who adopt a bottom-up approach "assume the responsibility hitherto ignored or not adequately dealt with the public bodies in charge[3]" (p. 42 European Commission). Instead, if social entrepreneurs follow a top-down approach, this means that they motivated in their behaviour and orientation by the type of welfare system and public policies.

The presence of durable top-down drivers for the birth of social entrepreneurship has two sides. On the one hand, it represents a breeding ground for entrepreneurial activities addressed to societal issues; on the other, it can weaken an entrepreneurial culture and feed excessive expectation for the public sector. In northern Europe, as it emerges from a study carried by the European Commission, there is a strong relationship between social enterprises and the public sector that has fostered a "state dependency".

The orientation towards others and the awareness of community issues make of social entrepreneurs *do-gooders*. They are part of human history, as Yunus (2017) outlines.

The concept of a social entrepreneur is not new: there are entrepreneurs that for decades have promoted strategies inspired to social issues (Welsh & Krueger, 2012). The importance covered by social entrepreneurship has grown thanks to the recognition of the relevance of this field by academicians and institutions, but also to the urgencies created by some catastrophic events: our mind goes to the hurricane Katrina in Louisiana, the tsunami in Asia in 2004, the HIV crisis in Africa, the earthquakes in Italy in 2009 and 2016, and the global COVID emergency in 2020. We should take a look at the social entrepreneurship and what happens during hard times.

Social Entrepreneurship in Hard Times

The role of social entrepreneurs is particularly helpful when communities are facing hard times. The advent of natural disasters or pandemic events

[3] In this specific case, we are referring to a report on social enterprises released by the European Commission. The report is available at the following link: MANCA IL LINK.

has increased the importance of social entrepreneurs within local communities. In some cases, they become the only available support for local people, a mean for surviving.

In the case of the hurricane Katrina in Louisiana, Chamlee-Wright & Storr (2009) have depicted the role of social entrepreneurs before and in the months following the disaster. We will start from the emerging insights from this case to describe the impact that social entrepreneurs can have on communities that are facing hard times.

Social entrepreneurs can help reduce the impact of a disaster; through the work they undertake before the accident, they can help in arising community's awareness towards the threats that might arise from natural settings. They can provide a means for making the living habitat safer. They can also inform communities on the importance of maintaining specific behaviours that can reduce the risk of being affected or damaged by a natural disaster.

Social entrepreneurs can provide support for managing the unexpected in various ways.

After a disaster, social entrepreneurs can create support for people in need.

In the months following the disaster, social entrepreneurs can "help to solve the collective action problem associated with deciding to return and rebuild, organise and engage in outreach, activism and advocacy on behalf of their communities, directly assist in rebuilding efforts and provide essential services" (Chamlee-Wright & Storr, 2009: 153).

The role played by social entrepreneurs is vital for the post-disaster phase; when people need to have a reason for coming back to the places where they lived, they need to find not only infrastructures and buildings but also a system of relationships. The role of entrepreneurs in this perspective is essential: social entrepreneurs help in keeping alive and reinforce social networks. Through their activity, they ensure people to find some relational elements of the community that people have left. Through social entrepreneurs, people can see their interests defended and represented in the dialogue with institutions, and this emerges in particular when entrepreneurs have notoriety among local communities.

The role of social entrepreneurship is pivotal in areas affected by earthquakes, such as the one that happened in Central Italy in 2016 (Pagliacci, Russo, & Sartori, 2017). That earthquake has required many efforts in rebuilding. Natural disasters represent a condition that requires the presence of people—such as social entrepreneurs—that can act as problem solvers or as facilitators: social entrepreneurs can reduce the distance between the organisational institution (local governmental bodies) and people. The work by Dutta (2017) represents an inspiration: it focuses on the dynamics connected to natural disasters happening in California between 1991 and 2010. With this paper, the author underlines the role of local community members and social entrepreneurs in helping people face emergencies and recovery. What is interesting in this work is that it appears that in some situations and places, it is easier to adopt a shared problem-solving approach. A key factor of success is the presence of a set of organising skills and frameworks that facilitate the contribution of community members to problem-solving. Some communities are more able to solve problems and have an active engagement in organising themselves to face difficulties because they have developed specific cultural competences and organisations that plan supporting activities over the long term.

Another interesting aspect emerges from the analysis of disaster management pursued by Chandra and Paras (2020). During disasters, different teams that bring together diverse expertise and interests have to cooperate. Technically, we refer to Emergency Recovery Groups (ERG) who put together people from different organisation bodies whose interest, sometimes, diverge. Yet, social entrepreneurs can act as facilitators and can ease the dialogue between different people and entities whose interests can conflict.

Challenges can happen even globally: epidemics or pandemic diseases can represent a threat to humanity. The recent experiences of Zika and Ebola have provided tools for assessing the devastating impact of the pandemic of COVID-19.

Pandemics are incredibly complex to manage: the forecasts about effects and impact can be vague, given the evolving scenario. Sometimes, as in the experience of COVID-19, the forcefulness of adopted measures was initially mitigated by partial knowledge of the characteristics of the virus. A similar condition has affected the effectiveness of the proposed solutions in the long range. In the cases of pandemics or aggressive epidemics, social entrepreneurs with their activities represent a lifeline. Social entrepreneurs can provide innovative solutions to societal problems, and they can be particularly helpful in the prevention of diseases and in supporting local communities in needs.

The work by Page et al. (2017) shows that the understanding of communities' emerging needs is crucial for organising adequate support to local stakeholders.

The ability to understand which are the emerging threats and compelling needs in local communities is a crucial issue for implementing practical actions promoted by social entrepreneurs. Therefore, social entrepreneurs need to be able to collect information from various sources and to analyse them critically, so as to have a deep understanding of the scenario that communities are living. It is essential, under this perspective, the type of linkage that social entrepreneurs have with communities is essential. For those coming from the voluntary sector (Leadbeater, 1997), it can be easier to gain direct information from people who are affected by the situation; therefore, social entrepreneurs must have a reliable set of information sources for performing a critical analysis of the inputs. The ability of social entrepreneurs to build a stable relationship with people based on mutual trust and a gained consensus facilitates entrepreneurs' access to information and knowledge. Then, they need to organise inputs into action.

Another essential role recognised to social entrepreneurs in the occasion of pandemic events and virus infections is prevention.

With the advent of Ebola, the organisations promoted by social entrepreneurs have actively contributed to the containment of the epidemy through their activities.

Madichie (2016) describes the role covered by social entrepreneurs during the Ebola epidemy in sub-Saharan Africa. What is interesting is that through their organisations, social entrepreneurs promote a new approach to life that includes some preventive measures that have had a decisive role in protecting people from Ebola. The work by Madichie (2016) focuses on the Global Soap Project (GSP), an organisation that was born from the idea of two social entrepreneurs, Derreck and Sarah Kayongo, in 2009. The couple decided to collect all little soap bars discarded at hotels and to use them for realising new soap bars. Through this project, people in refugee camps or other communities in need could have access to a supply that is basic for most of the people, but for them would be hardly accessible. With its activity, GSP has contributed to help reduce the impact of Ebola.

Social entrepreneurship can also become a mean for facing social and public health challenges. It is the case of obesity, one of the plagues that are affecting wealthy nations' health systems. Some scholars

(Smith, Calancie, & Ammerman, 2015) have investigated how social entrepreneurs can help reduce the incidence of obesity in the USA with their organisations. Although obesity prevention represents a core activity for a minimal number of social enterprises, many companies in the USA are committed to promoting healthy food consumption among local communities, by fostering a consumption model that can be defined as "local and healthy".

Some companies have tried to promote products or services that combine both healthy eating and physical activity. The problem with the relationship with food is multifaceted, and it covers several aspects: from the access to food, to the education about food consumption. There are social enterprises that operate to make food accessible to those categories of people that are in need: food banks are an example, and they work at a global level with different types of organisations (Waddock & Post, 1991).

The case explored by Santini and Cavicchi (2014) illustrates the activity of the food banks in Italy, and it describes how embedded social enterprises are in the Italian welfare system, and second the challenges that entrepreneurs of this reality have to face. In particular, the authors outline the link between some diseases such as obesity or diabetes and the poorest segments of the population. Therefore, the approach that social entrepreneurs who run this kind of organisations should have is not only to provide an answer to some basic needs (food access) but also to think about problems that could arise in the next future. In other words, the motto that often inspires some charity organisations is "give something is better than nothing". The aim is to provide a solution in the short run, but it is not foresight. This recalls the insights from Yunus (2017), who suggests that a charitable answer may not be the proper solution. Therefore, the vision of social entrepreneurs is a critical issue: the ability to design a sustainable strategy, oriented to the long run, is vital not only for the surviving but also for the effectiveness of the undertaken organisations.

Becoming Social Entrepreneurs

The future of social entrepreneurship seems particularly bright. There is a need for social entrepreneurship and social enterprises. Social entrepreneurs come from three main sectors (Leadbeater, 1997): public, private or voluntary.

In other words, someone who becomes a social entrepreneur can find a place in the public sector, or he can run a private company, or he/she can have roots in the voluntary sector. People from different fields, under this perspective, can have diverse backgrounds: they can have an in-depth knowledge of public companies, or they can have a vast experience of running a private company, or they can have relevant experience as volunteers in some local organisations and, in light of this, have an in-depth knowledge of the main problems affecting local communities.

Yunus (2017) clearly outlines the mechanisms that will foster the growth of social business enterprises and social entrepreneurs. The paths that social enterprises—and social entrepreneurs—can follow are different.

In some cases, existing companies will launch their social business enterprises, and they will become part of their social responsibility initiatives. In these circumstances, entrepreneurs can manage their social business enterprises by themselves or in partnership with others: the choice depends on several factors. They could have the need to outsource competencies, and so they decide to establish a collaboration with others, or they can manage everything on their own, internally.

The relationship with the existing company also defines the funding strategy of the social enterprise: it can happen to address a part of the annual profit of the leading company to the creation of social business enterprises. Another option is that companies create a social business enterprise investment fund.

Some investors can represent an opportunity for social entrepreneurs: the availability of funds can stimulate social entrepreneurs to run their social business.

Another reason that motivates entrepreneurs to operate in the social field affects the sphere of personal motivations: entrepreneurs might "feel and urge to try their creativity talent and management skill in establishing and running their own SBEs" (Yunus, 2017). The activity of a social entrepreneur is characterised by an extraordinary degree of creativity: through their creativity, social entrepreneurs can overcome problems and find innovative solutions. The challenges that social entrepreneurs must face are multifaceted, and they encourage the ability of people to remove barriers, to reduce the bureaucratic hurdles and, in general, to experiment.[4]

The presence of social start-ups varies across countries: a useful source of information is, to our knowledge, the Global Entrepreneurship Monitor (GEM) that depicts the global diffusion of entrepreneurship. The report shows that entrepreneurial activities and motivations change according to the location and to the type of economy that characterises the country. The visibility of social entrepreneurs has increased over time, given the growing recognition of companies: this aspect that emerges from the GEM report is not secondary. We have explored several issues of the report that is released on a yearly base. In the 2016 issue, we have noted an interesting aspect that is useful to understand the growth mechanisms of social entrepreneurship. Social enterprises and social entrepreneurs are becoming more and more visible, and people recognise that there is a considerable amount of individuals that are promoting business and organisations that have a positive impact on communities, and whose scope—that can be primary or not—is social. The ongoing recognition process undertaken by people reveals some interesting issues: in some countries, such as Luxemburg, visibility is low but social entrepreneurship is high; in others, such as the Philippines, the perceived profile is exceptionally high, but the "real" activity is not so high if compared to the rate of visibility. The emerging picture suggests that the perception of visibility is subjective. Still, entrepreneurs must work on promoting themselves and their activities to become much visible to communities and to be able not only to "market themselves", but also to make people aware about what they are doing.

Some Considerations

The theme of social entrepreneurs is intriguing and at the centre of a vivid academic debate.

We have seen that the definition of the scopes of the company is one of the pillars of academic research. The combined presence of personal drivers and economics drivers was one of the objects of the investigation

[4] "By removing artificial barriers to entry, reducing regulatory and bureaucratic hurdles and reducing government interventions so as not to crowd out entrepreneurial experimentation and creativity, social entrepreneurs (along with commercial entrepreneurs) can and will play key roles in community recovery" (Chamlee-Wright & Storr, 2009: 162).

by researchers. It is from the "real world" that the optimal combination emerges: the stories of entrepreneurs who promote social enterprises gave a new perspective to research in the field.

Therefore, the theme of social entrepreneurship has never been so relevant as in these times. The emergency of global health challenges, the occurring of natural disasters, as well as the dramatic problem of accessibility of resources cry for innovative solutions that can be pursued by social entrepreneurs. Yet, some questions emerge and deal with the adoption of successful models from the local scale to the global one. The debate is open, and it is immersed in a fluid and dynamic environment.

References

Alvord, S. H., Brown, L. D., & Letts, C. W. (2004). Social entrepreneurship and societal transformation: An exploratory study. *The Journal of Applied Behavioral Science, 40*(3), 260–282.

Chamlee-Wright, E., & Storr, V. H. (2009). The role of social entrepreneurship in post-Katrina community recovery. *International Journal of Innovation and Regional Development*, *2*(12), 149.

Chandra, Y., & Paras, A. (2020). Social entrepreneurship in the context of disaster recovery: Organizing for public value creation. *Public Management Review*, 1–22.

Dees, J. (2007). Taking social entrepreneurship seriously. *Society, 44*(3), 24–31.

Dutta, S. (2017). Creating in the crucibles of nature's fury: Associational diversity and local social entrepreneurship after natural disasters in California, 1991–2010. *Administrative Science Quarterly, 62*(3), 443–483.

Ebrashi, R. E. (2013). Social entrepreneurship theory and sustainable social impact. *Social Responsibility Journal, 9*(2), 188–209.

Ferreira, J. J., Fernandes, C. I., & Kraus, S. (2019). Entrepreneurship research: Mapping intellectual structures and research trends. *Review of Managerial Science, 13*(1), 181–205.

Hockerts, K. (2006). Entrepreneurial opportunity in social purpose business ventures. *Social Entrepreneurship*. Retrieved from https://link.springer.com/chapter/10.1057/9780230625655_10.

Kickul, J., Terjesen, S., Bacq, S., & Griffiths, M. (2012). Social business education: An interview with Nobel laureate Muhammad Yunus. A. *A Cademy of Management Learning & Education, 11*(3), 453–462.

Leadbeater, C. (1997). *The rise of the social entrepreneur*. London: England.

Madichie, N. O. (2016). The business of saving lives in Sub-Saharan Africa (SSA)—A social imperative? Insights from "The Global Soap Project". *Journal of Enterprising Communities: People and Places in the Global Economy, 10*(3), 321–342.

Mair, J., Robinson, J., & Hockerts, K. (2006). *Social entrepreneurship*. Retrieved from https://link.springer.com/content/pdf/10.1057/978 0230625655.pdf.

Marti, I. (2004). *Social entrepreneurship: What are we talking about?*. IESE Business School: A framework for future research.

Mirabella, R., & Young, D. R. (2012). The development of education for social entrepreneurship and nonprofit management: Diverging or converging paths? *Nonprofit Management and Leadership, 23*(1), 43–57.

Page, T. F., Williams, M. L., Cassella, G., Adler, J. L., & Amick, B. C., III. (2017). The impact of Zika on local businesses. *Disaster Prevention and Management: an International Journal, 26*(4), 452–457.

Pagliacci, F., Russo, M., & Sartori, L. (2017). Social innovation and natural disasters: The "Casa Italia" Plan. *Sociologia Urbana E Rurale, 113,* 87–102.

Persaud, A., Bayon, M., & Cartmell, S. (2018). Social entrepreneurship research: A bibliometric analysis. *Academy of Management Proceedings, 2018*(1), 15510.

Roger, M., & Osberg, S. (2007). Social entrepreneurship: The case for definition. *Stanford Social Innovation Review* (Spring), 28–39.

Santini, C., & Cavicchi, A. (2014). The adaptive change of the Italian Food Bank foundation: A case study. *British Food Journal, 116*(9), 1446–1459. https://doi.org/10.1108/BFJ-06-2014-0201.

Smith, T., Calancie, L., & Ammerman, A. (2015). Social entrepreneurship for obesity prevention: What are the opportunities? *Current Obesity Reports, 4*(3), 311–318.

Sullivan Mort, G., Weerawardena, J., & Carnegie, K. (2003). Social entrepreneurship: Towards conceptualisation. *International Journal of Nonprofit and Voluntary Sector Marketing, 8*(1), 76–88.

Swanson, L. A., & Di Zhang, D. (2010). The social entrepreneurship zone. *Journal of Nonprofit & Public Sector Marketing, 22*(2), 71–88.

Waddock, S. A., & Post, J. E. (1991). Social entrepreneurs and catalytic change. *Public Administration Review, 51*(5), 401.

Welsh, D. H. B., & Krueger, N. (2012). The evolution of social entrepreneurship: What have we learned? *Journal of Technology Management in China, 7*(3), 270–290.

Yunus, M. (2017). Social business entrepreneurs are the solution. In *The future makers* (pp. 219–225). Routledge.

CHAPTER 4

Who Are the Good Entrepreneurs?

Abstract In the research field of entrepreneurship, many niches are emerging. This work focuses on new definitions of entrepreneurs: sustainable entrepreneur; enviropreneur; ecopreneur. The work will illustrate how the changes in corporate culture, economic environment and society have created the space for new types of entrepreneurs. The chapter underlines the role of empowerment, innovation and institutions for the emerging of entrepreneurs who emphasize sustainable, social and green issues when operating. Then, a reflection on how personality and motivations shape entrepreneurship is provided.

Keywords Sustainable entrepreneurship · Environmental entrepreneurship · Enviropreneurship · Ecological entrepreneurship · Green entrepreneurship · Ecopreneurship · Empowerment · Personal motivations · Personality

Introduction

We have explored the role that social entrepreneurs have in the pursuit of the good. Besides social entrepreneurs, there are other types of entrepreneurs whose focus is on sustainability, ecology and environment. In this chapter, we will provide an overview of the main typologies of entrepreneurs that deal with sustainable or ecological issues. Each of these

C. Santini, *The Good Entrepreneur*,
https://doi.org/10.1007/978-3-030-59332-2_4

new types of entrepreneurs represents a research niche, that is evolving, and that is growing. To understand the determinants (or drivers) of the growing presence of such entrepreneurs allows us to evaluate if there is a set of conditions that ideally promote the booming of environmental and sustainable concerns among entrepreneurs. Thus, from the literature, it emerges that sometimes it can be arduous to distinguish between the different typologies of entrepreneurs. We will focus on the phenomenon of the rising of environmental concern among entrepreneurs from an academic perspective. With the growing interest in ecological practices by entrepreneurs, scholars have matured the need to distinguish the features of each type of entrepreneurs.

Drivers

Ecological and sustainable issues have progressively gained space in entrepreneurship, and they currently find a place in book texts and articles that focus on entrepreneurship (Schaper, 2002).

Academic interest for sustainable and ecological impact on entrepreneurship is motivated by many factors. Many reasons explain the rise of entrepreneurship with an environmental and sustainable orientation; the emerging framework is highly complex. According to Gast (2017), the reasons why entrepreneurs become sustainable are four: there are motives linked to regulation, to public concern, to expected competitive advantage and to top management convincement. This descriptive approach helps us to understand which are the features of this kind of entrepreneurs. The motivations can be external to the company and entrepreneurs: the presence of regulation and norms can promote entrepreneurship. At the same time, personal motivations can improve entrepreneurial orientation towards environmental concern. A regulatory framework that forces firms to become sustainable can promote green entrepreneurship.

We will describe some of the significant issues that affect the development of sustainable, environmental, green or eco-entrepreneurs, and, as a consequence, the growth of research in the field.

Changes in Corporate Culture and Society

First of all, in entrepreneurial and top management culture gain relevance, the impact that companies have on societies. The reshaping of corporate and entrepreneurial culture and the rising of awareness towards the pitfalls of decision-making have put sustainable issues under the spotlight.

At a global level, we can also observe the establishment of a link between environmental objectives and economic, social and political development (Selman, 1998). The global debate on sustainability has involved, through an empowerment process, people, and it has brought sustainability at the centre of the economic debate.

Entrepreneurs have started to conduct their businesses to address stakeholders' concerns on sustainable and environmental problems (Mukonza, 2016).

Therefore, entrepreneurs with years of experience have begun to take into consideration—if they have never done before—the importance of sustainable practices, given their relevance to people. A category of nascent entrepreneurs took inspiration from the ecological and green concernment of some stakeholders, and they have started businesses that emphasize the importance of being sustainable (Schick, Marxen, & Freimann, 2002). Scholars debate if it is easier to develop a sustainable corporate culture from the early beginning of a firm or to implement it during the life cycle of the venture. Companies show different degree of ecological orientation: Schick et al. (2002) have provided a description of start-up orientation that offers some useful insights for examining all the companies. Corporate culture can be eco dedicated, open or reluctant. Eco-dedicated companies usually employ environmentally friendly business practices, and ecological orientation plays a vital role in a venture's culture. Eco-open companies partially adopt eco-friendly business practices, while eco-reluctant companies choose to take an environmental orientation to accomplish to a set of rules established by institutions.

Studies show waves of the greening of the industry: for instance, the development of management systems and practices—the Environmental Management System (EMS), the Eco-Management and Audit Scheme (EMAS) or ISO 14001—has actively contributed to diffuse environmentally friendly business practices among companies. Some authors, anyway, are critical about the positive effect that codified green business practices can have in shaping an eco-friendly corporate culture. In particular, Schick et al. (2002) underline: "However, the positive environmental effects of EMSs are rather small (see, e.g. Dyllick & Hamschmidt 2000; Morrow & Rondinelli 2002), and the normal state of organizational practice does not match state of the art in organizational theory. EMSs are expert-based systems in which corporate environmental care is dictated in a top-down way. It is rare to find substantial changes in corporate culture arising from the adoption of EMSs. In practice, the implementation of more sustainable business measures into an existing organizational culture is often an arduous and lengthy process, resulting in conventional additional environmental conservation measures that do not reach beyond daily operating procedures" (p. 60).

We can say, that in general, top-down approaches to green practices have limited effectiveness in shaping an environmentally friendly corporate culture. The changing of corporate culture can be challenging, and it requires a high degree of interactions among internal stakeholders and an in-depth knowledge of existing culture and areas of changes.[1]

Therefore, we can say that environmental orientation progressively became part of corporate culture, and it helped to foster entrepreneurial awareness towards green and sustainable issues.

The Role of Empowerment

Empowerment is an overused term by policymakers: it can sound vague since it refers to some conceptual ideas. When talking about empowerment, we refer to a bottom-up approach, that is primarily based on participation and trust. The first step is the achievement of an awareness of personal choices and role within society. The establishment of a trusted network among people amplifies the pitfalls of individual actions. With a specific referral to sustainable practices and development, empowerment plays a significant role. One of the inspiring principles of empowerment is that change is interactive (Lyons, Smuts, & Stephens, 2001). Sustainable development is "the ability acquired and held by communities over time, to initiate and control development, thus enabling communities to participate more effectively in their destiny" (p. 1237). Some studies, like the

[1] The issue of corporate cultural change is at the center of an endless debate. We have found particularly enlightening the insights from Hassard and Sharifi (1989) who write "Change is easier when the change process involves only surface-level behavioural norms; i.e. because members themselves can suggest what behaviours are required for success today as opposed to those required yesterday. Managing the deepest layers of culture requires a participative approach, a derivative of Theory Y: because top management, with or without the help of consultants, cannot dictate changes in assumptions about human nature and the business environment, they can only set appropriate parameters. A top-down approach to cultural change may be feasible when either a single corporate culture exists, or where the focus is upon changing norms and not assumptions" (p. 628).

one previously cited, explore the role that the empowerment process has in shaping people's culture. Some issues, such as sustainability or social justice, can benefit from an empowerment approach since they look for a large basin of consensus and they need to convince every single person that they can "make the difference". The relevance of empowerment is under everybody's eyes when we think about the process of awareness and adoption of sustainable and eco-friendly behaviours by citizens. It is one of the principles that regulate movements run by young activists: we refer to the examples of Greta Thunberg and Malala Yousafzai (Skrzypczak, Pelzer, & Süli, 2019). United Nations have recognized the role that the empowerment process has in the education of youths (Holmberg & Alvinius, 2020) with specific reference to health or sustainable practices.

Some case studies show that empowering entrepreneurs can improve sustainable practices: it is the case of female rural Amazonian entrepreneurs described by Mello and Schmink (2017) or the experience pursued by women in Gujarat (Haugh & Talwar, 2016). Yet, in our opinion, there is no doubt that empowerment has fostered the interest in green and ecological issues.

Organisations and Institutions

Institutions and policymakers have supported through their policies the diffusion of some practices that preserve resources and reduce ecological impact; there is no doubt that this approach shown by politicians has promoted entrepreneurial attention to sustainable and green issues.

We have already mentioned the role pursued by policymakers for the development of a system of norms that could improve the adoption of green practices (we refer, for example, to EMS or EMAS). Besides policies that will enhance the diffusion of environmentally friendly business practices, organisations and institutions have facilitated the growth of green or sustainable entrepreneurship. Institutions and governments had to consider the problems of social equity and resource availability: they aim to reduce social inequalities and guarantee access to resources. The importance of sustainable and balanced management of environmental and financial resources to face inequality is fully recognized not only by scholars (Shrivastava, 2011) but also by institutions and organisations who see in green entrepreneurship a mean for facing social challenges. Yet, a consensus towards green, sustainable and environmental issues progressively affirmed worldwide and gained importance in policymaking.

The above-described scenario has facilitated to entrepreneurs the transpose of some personal values and commitment (such as a green orientation) in strategy making.

Then, the availability of organisations and institution that support and promote sustainable issues has created a breeding ground for the diffusion of a type of entrepreneur who blinks the eye to these topics.

Innovation

The urgency of adopting new production and transformation practices that reduce environmental impact has nurtured the diffusion of eco-innovation.

When we talk about eco-innovation, we refer to "innovative products and process that reduce the environmental impacts". The terms are often employed in conjunction with *eco-efficiency* and *eco-design* (Sarkar, 2013: 172). By introducing the issue of eco-innovation, our aim is not to provide an exhaustive overview of the phenomenon. Still, we want to outline the emerging of a vast amount of entrepreneurial activities that brought to innovative output in this field. In other words, the opening of spaces for eco-innovation has fostered the development of entrepreneurs whose aim is to create innovative eco-solutions.

The literature on innovation and its determinants is endless: scholars confirm that the degree of innovativeness of a country depends, among various factors, on the presence of entrepreneurs who are particularly proactive in the development of innovative start-ups. Theoretical insights find a confirmation in field research: the National Innovation System Analysis (NIS) developed by the European Commission highlights that the development of innovative systems is linked to the presence of structural economic indicators (demand for innovations, industry structure, open economy) and sociocultural institutional indicators (finance system, receptiveness to new ideas, social equity, labour market and entrepreneurial attitude).

In our perspective, innovation indeed grows where there are illuminated entrepreneurs, but we can say that entrepreneurs might find particularly inspiring those environments where the degree of innovation is high. In our opinion, areas or communities that are particularly responsive to green change can stimulate innovative green entrepreneurship. Entrepreneurs who are interested in developing creative green business ideas can benefit from the presence of other start-ups who, with their innovative products or services, have contributed to boosting an orientation towards innovation. Entrepreneurs can feel a sense of consensus about the way they operate and can be motivated in pursuing their projects because they understand that the environment where they live and work is ready to know what they have to say. In other words, innovation can generate an openness in local cultures and communities for further ideas.

Personal Traits and Motivations

Much literature focuses on the role that personal traits and motivations can have in sustainable or green entrepreneurship.

In some cases, authors recognize a linkage between the nascent entrepreneurs and some social movements. In the case of ecopreneurs, for example, some scholars acknowledge the role that some social movements—more specifically ecological movements—have had since the 1970s in shaping entrepreneurs' motivations (Beveridge & Guy, 2005). Yet, in this case, the sense of alignment between personal motivations and the values promoted by social movements influences entrepreneur's decisions: entrepreneurs feel a sense of sharing of their convictions, and they also perceive the support that emerges from social movements.

The literature has widely explored the relevancy of personal traits and motivations in entrepreneurial behaviour. We have previously highlighted, in this book, the importance of personality and personal characteristics in the shaping of entrepreneurial behaviour.

Furthermore, the literature suggests observing the interactions between entrepreneurs' personal and organisational qualities and their economic social and political (or technological) context. When there is an external pressure that leads to the adoption of environmental practices, it is clear that top management or entrepreneurs' traits and motivations play a significative role in the overall degree of sustainability of their companies.

Background research has highlighted the importance given to personal traits in the definition of green or sustainable orientation among entrepreneurs (Santini, 2017). In general, scholars suggest that a pro-environmental attitude simplifies the adoption of pro-environmental decisions.

The work by Schaltegger and Wagner (2011) provides an exhaustive description of the set of motivations that characterise the different types of entrepreneurs. For ecopreneurs, the core motivation is to contribute to solve environmental problems and to create economic value. Social entrepreneurs aim to address societal challenges and create value for society, and sustainable entrepreneurs' goal is to solve societal and environmental problems through the realisation of a successful business. We will see later, more in details, the characteristics of each type of entrepreneur.

New Types of Entrepreneurs

The growing attention to environmental and sustainable issues gave a chance to entrepreneurs to put at the centre of their choices their commitment to adopt ethical behaviours for preserving resources. Researchers gave space to new features in entrepreneurship. In the previous paragraphs, we have employed terms like sustainability, ecology, environment as synonyms; scholars have made some distinctions among the different types of entrepreneurs. Scholars have progressively built a taxonomy by observing the diffusion of specific entrepreneurial behaviours that lead back to particular typologies of entrepreneurs.

Initially, there the idea of an entrepreneur interested in pursuing sustainable or green behaviour and it was encompassing many characteristics, such as the commitment to adopt sustainable practices; the intention to preserve resources; a personal vision about green or ecological issues and its role in spreading the gospel of sustainability among people; and so forth.

As some scholars have outlined (Nair & Ganesh, 2013; Ndubisi, 2009), the initial approach to "green practices and sustainable businesses" was to consider isolated from the set of implemented practices. Then, scholars have realized the importance of understanding the linkage between practices and business philosophy and culture.

Publications started to boom, and the different characteristics among entrepreneurs slowing emerged.

In our opinion, the difficulties in distinguishing among different typologies of entrepreneurs derive from the novelty of the research field and its continuous growth.

Scholars have provided a different definition for green entrepreneur, eco-entrepreneur, environmental entrepreneur and sustainable entrepreneur. For each of the categories, we will provide a description and an overview of emerging insights from academic research.

There is a multitude of terms and definitions, such as ecopreneurship, environmental entrepreneurship, green entrepreneurship and sustainable entrepreneurship. It is hard, sometimes, to distinguish between the different typologies.

Green and Environmental Entrepreneurship

What characterises this type of entrepreneurs is to be green: he/she makes its business green or gets into a green business.

Green and environmental entrepreneurs are, to our opinion, very similar. As we will see later in this book, there is a tendency to implement neologisms that identify research niches. The term "green" associated with the word entrepreneur is more general than the name "enviropreneur".

A first attempt to define what green entrepreneurship is can start from the analysis of green businesses and green activities. OECD shows two approaches for the definition of green entrepreneurship: "it could be defined in terms of the technology used for production in any sector of the economy, or in terms of the sector's firms are active in, in which case our attention is restricted to parts of the economy producing specific types of output. The former is sometimes referred to as a process approach in defining green business, while the latter as an output approach" (pp. 24–25).

The above-provided definition doesn't include ethical issues or personal motivations.

In the definition released by the European Commission, a green entrepreneur provides ecological awareness to the firm.

Scholars define green entrepreneurship as "a method for managing natural resources" (Allen, 2008). As we can see, the definition is extensive.

A solution to provide some less generic definition could be to highlight the activities that green entrepreneur should perform. In other words, a green entrepreneur can be someone who pursues green activities. A new debate opens on the understanding of what a green business is and the OECD report on green entrepreneurship[2] provides useful insights: according to the report, are green all those entrepreneurs who operate

[2] The OECD report is available at the following link: https://www.oecd-ilibrary.org/docserver/9789264097711-4-en.pdf?expires=1589099633&id=id&accname=guest&checksum=0E75BE0F3F1CA1E547047AEBD7DD098C.

in companies in the so-called pollution management fields (production of equipment and specific materials for air pollution control, wastewater and solid waste management, environmental monitoring, analysis and assessment, and so forth); in the cleaner technologies and product field; or in the resource management field (production of equipment, technology, specific materials, services, construction and installation for water supply, indoor management, renewable energy plant and so forth).

A reflection upon the management of natural resources by green entrepreneurs leads to further inquiries: "how natural resource-dependent communities, which often deal with persistent poverty, can harness the initiative of local entrepreneurs to create sustainable, lucrative businesses" (Allen, 2008). Once again, it emerges how definitions are fluid: the borders of green entrepreneurship inevitably fade into sustainable entrepreneurship.

Yet, the term green can be employed in a relative sense or an absolute sense (Isaak, 2017; Walley & Taylor, 2002): some businesses are green since their foundation—and they show an "absolute" implementation of the term green—and activities that turn green. At the same time, there are entrepreneurs who since the beginning are characterised by a strong commitment to environmental practices and others who became "green" after they recognize the relevancy of being green. The motivations that boost in entrepreneurs an ecological concern can be multiple: they can feel institutional pressure, or they can perceive the importance of their role in the changing process of the society, or they can recognize the emerging commercial opportunities. In any of the above-described cases, entrepreneurs decide to become green.

According to the literature, ecopreneurs are founders of *green* business (Isaak, 2017; Walley & Taylor, 2002). Following the emerging insights from the research, we can define as green entrepreneurs those who conduct green businesses; thus, among the classifications of green companies, scholars—see, for example, Walley and Taylor (2002) or Holt (2011)—emphasize the one published by Eastwood, Eaton, Guyer, and Stark (2001). The authors outline eleven different types of green business that go from pollution control and energy conservation to research and education.

This kind of entrepreneurs has a notable environmental motivation that inspires their choices and behaviours.

The model proposed by Walley and Taylor (2002) describes what the main activities and characteristics of green entrepreneurs are. The authors distinguish four types of entrepreneurs: ***innovative opportunists, visionary champions, ethical mavericks and hoc enviropreneurs.***

In this taxonomy, we note that the authors employ the term enviropreneurs to indicate a unique typology of green entrepreneurs. In this case, we refer to accidental green entrepreneurs, who are inspired by personal relations and network to implement green practices within their business. What are they seeking is financial value, and in their view, being green can help in achieving superior financial performances.

The innovative opportunist in response to regulation pressure adopts green practices; they are animated even by a high economic orientation. The motivations are entirely different from those that inspire a visionary champion entrepreneur: in this case, the entrepreneur, since the foundation of its business, adopts sustainable practices. A singular character is the ethical maverick. Ethical mavericks adopt sustainable and green practices because they are part of a network (of friends or relatives) or they have had some experiences that have changed their vision of the world. The pressure of regulation is soft in ethical mavericks who tend to create alternative-style start-ups.

Ecopreneurship

There are many definitions of ecopreneurship. In general, ecopreneurship combines two words: ecological and entrepreneurship, and the introduction of the term dates back to the ecological movement. This is one of the reasons why ecopreneurs are often confused with ecological activists. As for other typologies of entrepreneurs, it is challenging to find a unique definition of ecopreneurship. We are dealing with a complex issue, and since there is a lack of academic consensus about what constitutes an entrepreneur, it is even harder to define what ecopreneurship is (Santini, 2017). As for all the other typologies that we have previously outlined and that we will see forward, the problems are the same. Kirkwood, Walton, Kirkwood, and Walton (2010) suggest that ecopreneurs are entrepreneurs who found new businesses based on the principles of sustainability.

Ecopreneurs focus on environmental performance rather than on social performance (Schaltegger & Wagner, 2011), and "they pay less attention to sustainability performance (that combines social and environmental issues), which is seldom perceived as a core business goal" (Santini, 2017: 4). Ecopreneurship can be defined as "entrepreneurship through environmental lenses" (Schaltegger, 2010: 78). Some new traits of ecopreneurs emerge from the work by Schaltegger (2010), who highlights that one of the ecopreneurial purposes is to achieve a considerable market share: accordingly, to this perspective, ecopreneurs are highly motivated to reach the widest audience as possible. This, in our view, is aligned with the traits of activism in ecopreneurs, as previously outlined. Yet, the description provided by Schaltegger (2010) solves the dilemma of choosing between making profits and pursuing personal inspirations. In some works, we find traces of the discussion "choose profits or motivation" (Linnanen, 2005), but, by focusing on commitments, others highlight the importance of spreading the message of ecology to the masses: those entrepreneurs see in ecology one of the core inspiring principles of their companies. To pose at the centre of their businesses, such principles lead entrepreneurs to implement ecological practices (Santini, 2017; Schaltegger, 2002).[3]

When we talk about ecopreneurship, we are used to employing synonyms, such as sustainable or green orientation instead of ecological orientation. Yet, sometimes, the borders between different definitions seem to fade. When analysing the literature, anyway, we observe that the implementation of this neologism is growing up to the point of introducing other specific sub-categories. It is the case of "shecopreneurship", introduced in 2011 (Poldner, Branzei, & Steyaert, 2011). In other words, the literature is still growing and evolving.

Sustainable Entrepreneurship

Another type of entrepreneur is the sustainable entrepreneur.

We can provide a definition that basically, follows the others: a sustainable entrepreneur—or sustainopreneur—is an entrepreneur who is motivated by sustainable purposes.

Given the broad concept of sustainability that includes several perspectives (the ecological one, but also the social and economic ones), a sustainopreneur can operate on various levels that touch the different spheres of sustainability.

Scholars have investigated the niche of sustainable entrepreneurship. The work by Sarango, Santos, and Hormiga (2018) provides a state of the art of background research on sustainopreneurship as a research field.

[3]We suggest to carefully read the work by Schaltegger, published in 2010: the author describes "ecopreneurial positioning" and he explains how many different "degrees" of ecopreneurship we can find.

Sarango et al. (2018) underline that the initial focus of the research was on environmental problems and solutions, and it evolved to include all the dimensions of the concept of sustainability.

Many factors contribute to define entrepreneurial sustainability orientation: there is no doubt that individual factors play a pivotal role in determining companies' sustainable goals (Kuckertz & Wagner, 2010; Schaltegger & Wagner, 2017).

Sarango et al. (2018) describe what the main aims of a sustainable entrepreneur are: "(1) be motivated by identities based on both commercial and ecological logics; (2) prioritize commercial and/or ecological goals; and (3) approach stakeholders in a broadly inclusive, exclusive, or co-created manner to acquire financial resources through crowdfunding, because sustainable entrepreneurs do not seem to be ready to respond to the challenges or to take any risks by investing in green business, but also that the government and educational institutions do not recognize their own role and the need of supporting the development of green entrepreneurship" (p. 11).

Some Considerations

We are witnessing to the growth of some research niches in the field of entrepreneurship. In some cases, as for entrepreneurship or ecopreneurship, we see that research is at an embryo phase, but it is growing: we observe a shift from the implementation of generic terms to specific definitions that tend to delimit some particular phenomena.

We can say that a hierarchical order can organize the typology of entrepreneurs presented in this chapter. The concept of sustainable entrepreneurship seems more extensive, and it includes all the other typologies of entrepreneurs described in the section.

As literature grows, scholars have dedicated attention to make further distinctions, and specific categories have risen. The birth of smaller research niches goes along with the growth of entrepreneurs' orientation towards specific sustainable practices.

Future research should investigate the dynamics of the above-described research niches. Will they survive in the future or will be incorporated by the field of sustainable entrepreneurship? In our view, as long as entrepreneurs will show interest in green and sustainable business practices—whatever their motives are—it is reasonable to suppose that research niches will grow. It is essential to underline that, as outlined by some scholars (Santini, 2017), there is a lack of field research. When we have explored the literature, we have observed that most of the studies aimed to provide classifications, taxonomies or indicators for understanding what the distinguishing traits of each type of entrepreneur are. We see some confusion about who is who; this is, in our view, because the object of study is still in progress. It is hard to say how many years does it take to a research niche to get its definition and development. Yet, we have learned from the previous sections of the book that entrepreneurship is still looking for its legitimacy, so we must be patient and observe these promising research niches.

References

Allen, J. (2008). Green entrepreneurship: A method for managing natural resources? *Society and Natural Resources, 21*(9), 828–844. https://doi.org/10.1080/08941920701612917.

Beveridge, R., & Guy, S. (2005). The rise of the eco-preneur and the messy world of environmental innovation. *Local Environment, 10*(6), 665–676.

Eastwood, D., Eaton, M., Guyer, C., & Stark, T. (2001). An examination of employment change in Northern Ireland's environmental industry, 1993–2003. *European Environment, 11*(4), 197–210.

Gast, J. (2017). Doing business in a green way: A systematic review of the ecological sustainability entrepreneurship literature and future research directions. *Journal of Cleaner Production, 147*, 44–56. https://doi.org/10.1016/j.jclepro.2017.01.065.

Hassard, J., & Sharifi, S. (1989). Corporate culture and strategic change. *Journal of General Management, 15*(2), 4–19.

Haugh, H. M., & Talwar, A. (2016). Linking social entrepreneurship and social change: The mediating role of empowerment. *Journal of Business Ethics, 133*(4), 643–658.

Holmberg, A., & Alvinius, A. (2020). Children's protest in relation to the climate emergency: A qualitative study on a new form of resistance promoting political and social change. *Childhood, 27*(1), 78–92.

Holt, D. (2011). Where are they now? tracking the longitudinal evolution of environmental businesses from the 1990s. *Business Strategy and the Environment, 20*(4), 238–250. https://doi.org/10.1002/bse.697.

Isaak, R. (2017). *Green logic: Ecopreneurship, theory and ethics*. Retrieved from https://www.taylorfrancis.com/books/9781351283168.

Kirkwood, J., Walton, S., Kirkwood, J., & Walton, S. (2010). *What motivates ecopreneurs to start businesses?* https://doi.org/10.1108/13552551011042799.

Kuckertz, A., & Wagner, M. (2010). The influence of sustainability orientation on entrepreneurial intentions: Investigating the role of business experience. *Journal of Business Venturing*, *25*(524–539).

Linnanen, L. (2005). An insider's experiences with environmental entrepreneurship. *Making ecopreneurs: Developing sustainable* .... Retrieved from https://books.google.com/books?hl=en&lr=&id=8AMfDAAAQBAJ&oi=fnd&pg=PA109&dq=ecopreneurship&ots=H1QxEOuoLK&sig=yQJbSzsyyLxrZHLoG9yCO_aWO4Q.

Lyons, M., Smuts, C., & Stephens, A. (2001). Participation, empowerment and sustainability: (How) do the links work? *Urban Studies, 38*(8), 1233–1251.

Mello, D., & Schmink, M. (2017). Amazon entrepreneurs: Women's economic empowerment and the potential for more sustainable land use practices. *Women's Studies International Forum, 65*(November), 28–36.

Mukonza, C. (2016). *Analysis of factors influencing green entrepreneurship in South Africa.*

Nair, S., & Ganesh, C. (2013). Reasons and influences of the practice of environmental marketing. *Journal of Management Research, 13*(2), 77–88. Retrieved from http://search.proquest.com/docview/1466137809/.

Ndubisi, N. (2009). Green Entrepreneurship (GE) and Green Value Added (GVA): A conceptual framework. *International Journal of Entrepreneurship, 13*, 21–34. Retrieved from https://www.scopus.com/inward/record.uri?partnerID=HzOxMe3b&scp=77953473850&origin=inward.

Poldner, K., Branzei, O., & Steyaert, C. (2011). Shecopreneuring: stitching global ecosystems in the ethical fashion industry. In A. Marcus, P. Shrivastava, S. Sharma, & S. Pogutz (Eds.), *Cross-sector leadership for the green economy: Integrating research and practice on sustainable enterprise* (pp. 157–173). https://doi.org/10.1057/9781137015891_9.

Santini, C. (2017). Ecopreneurship and ecopreneurs: Limits. *Trends and Characteristics.*

Sarango-Lalangui, P., Santos, J. L. S., & Hormiga, E. (2018). The development of sustainable entrepreneurship research field. *Sustainability.* Retrieved from https://www.mdpi.com/2071-1050/10/6/2005.

Sarkar, A. N. (2013). Promoting eco-innovations to leverage sustainable development of eco-industry and green growth. *European Journal of Sustainable Development, 2*(1), 171–224.

Schaltegger, S. (2002). A framework for ecopreneurship: Leading bioneers and environmental managers to ecopreneurship. *Greener Management International, 38*, 45–58. https://doi.org/10.9774/GLEAF.3062.2002.su.00006.

Schaltegger, S. (2010). A framework and typology. *Making ecopreneurs: Developing sustainable* .... Retrieved from https://books.google.com/books?hl=en&lr=&id=AIRILhGp3yUC&oi=fnd&pg=PA75&dq=ecopreneurship&ots=bGnJ0Iwbym&sig=AmqT5PnSApNL1ZAIDr1UKM7A5tk.

Schaltegger, S., & Wagner, M. (2011). Sustainable entrepreneurship and sustainability innovation: Categories and interactions. *Business strategy and the ….* Retrieved from https://onlinelibrary.wiley.com/doi/abs/10.1002/bse.682.

Schaltegger, S., & Wagner, M. (2017). *Managing the business case for sustainability: The integration of social, environmental and economic performance.* Retrieved from https://www.taylorfrancis.com/books/e/9781351280525.

Schaper, M. (2002). The challenge of environmental responsibility and sustainable development: Implications for SME and entrepreneurship academics. *Radical Changes in the World: Will SMEs Soar or ….* Retrieved from https://www.researchgate.net/profile/Michael_Schaper/publication/260387357_The_challenge_of_environmental_responsibility_and_sustainable_development_Implications_for_SME_and_entrepreneurship_academics/links/54ececa20cf2465f53306ac8.pdf.

Schick, H., Marxen, S., & Freimann, J. (2002). Sustainability issues for start-up entrepreneurs. *Greener Management International, 38,* 59–70.

Selman, P. (1998). Local agenda 21: Substance or spin? *Journal of Environmental Planning and Management, 41,* 533–553.

Shrivastava, P. (2011). Enterprise sustainability 2.0: Aesthetics of sustainability. In *The oxford handbook of business and the natural environment.* Retrieved from http://oxfordhandbooks.com/view/10.1093/oxfordhb/9780199584451.001.0001/oxfordhb-9780199584451-e-35.

Skrzypczak, J., Pelzer, B., & Süli, O. (2019). Youth activists for our health. *The Lancet*, *394*(10213), 1992. Retrieved from http://search.proquest.com/docview/2319466452/.

Walley, E. E., & Taylor, D. W. (2002). Opportunists, champions, mavericks…? *Greener management international.* Retrieved from https://www.jstor.org/stable/pdf/greemanainte.38.31.pdf.

CHAPTER 5

Research Niches and Trends

Abstract This chapter describes the process of niche formation in the research field of entrepreneurship. It also provides a critical reflection on the usefulness of bibliometric analysis for understanding trends and future direction of research. We analyse the role of grey literature in the development of niche research field, with particular attention to the categories of ecopreneurs, social, green and environmental entrepreneurs.

Keywords Research niche · Bibliometric approach · Literature review · Grey literature · Ecopreneurship · Green entrepreneurship · Environmental entrepreneurship · Enviropreneurship, ecological entrepreneurship · Social entrepreneurship · Research niche

Introduction

The field of entrepreneurship is in continuous evolution, as we have previously outlined. Scholars employ bibliometric analysis for understanding trends and future directions of research. The availability of some analytical tools has fostered the diffusion of quantitative analysis of the literature. Literature reviews help, among the various purposes, to build a foundation, to show knowledge advancements, and to support findings interpretation and the conceptualisation of studies (Rocco & Plakhotnik, 2009).

C. Santini, *The Good Entrepreneur*,
https://doi.org/10.1007/978-3-030-59332-2_5

Literature reviews can follow various methodologies: we can first perform a distinction in qualitative, quantitative and mixed methods.

A literature review suggests if a topic is researchable, and it highlights how close it is to previous studies.

In this book, we have described the birth process of niches in entrepreneurship. We know that in business, niches evolve and can achieve considerable dimensions: the same happens in research since niches experienced a growth in the number of publications. In some cases, the number of published articles—that focus on a specific theme—grew, and the research issue from a marginal niche became a vast topic.

Yet, sometimes concepts could overlap: we have seen how difficult it is to distinguish among *green, eco* or *enviro* entrepreneur. Some research spaces that were initially micro-niches, with the evolving of the discipline, merged and disappeared.

Therefore, a careful observation of indexes and science maps can provide useful insights into what is happening in research.

Tools and Indexes

The evaluation of research trends needs a definition of tools and indexes for performing an adequate analysis.

The evaluation can outline scholars' impact or the impact that an article has on research.

There are many indexes, and each index provides different information.

Besides Impact Factor, many interesting indexes emerged over time: the Immediacy Index, the Cited Half-Life or the Rate of Cites Index provide us information about the performance, the quality or the validity of an article. The advent of open access has created further space for newer indexes. We observe the implementation of indexes such as the Usage Factor or the Web Impact Factor. Webometrics, a new field in bibliometrics, arises.

Scholars can also gain useful insights from science mapping or bibliometric mapping. With science mapping, scholars can understand which are the connections among different aspects of research. Science mapping represents intellectual connections and dynamism of research (Cobo, López-Herrera, Herrera-Viedma, & Herrera, 2011b).

Networks in research are critical: scholars share ideas and collaborate through networks. When reading a paper, it is interesting to see who the authors are citing. We can also use network analysis to highlight overlaps in research or to identify the most influential authors in the field. The units of study can be authors, documents, publications or keywords: we can find co-citation or co-author analysis, for example (Cobo et al., 2011a).

Cobo et al. (2011a) provide a taxonomy of the main bibliometric techniques; following their example, we have summarized all the types of analysis according to the typology of documents to explore and the study to perform (Table 5.1).

Science mapping is helpful in a literature review. The availability of many softwares with specific characteristics (Cobo et al., 2011b) has facilitated the implementation of science mapping.

Bibliometric analysis and science mapping have registered a diffusion among disciplines where literature is in continuous expansion, and there is a vast number of articles to examine.

Entrepreneurship has benefited from bibliometrics and science mapping.

We have performed a quick analysis of the results from SCOPUS, and we have found 141 documents that deal with the topics *entrepreneurship* and *bibliometric analysis.* Most of them are articles, and the highest concentration of publications is in the period 2016–2019, with a peak of 44 published documents in 2019. An exciting aspect concerns the role that foundations play in the promotion of this type of research: many published articles are endorsed or supported by some institutions. The explanation is in the social role of the discipline, as we have previously outlined in this book. Furthermore, we should also underline that some research centres or universities appear as particularly prolific in this research field. Besides the interest shown by some research groups, there is another explanation. Some departments have developed programmes for science mapping or bibliometric analysis, and they are interested in promoting their diffusion.

We should underline that some mapping software tools are available under commercial licences (Cobo et al., 2011b); the availability of open-source software has created new space for this kind of research. We are referring to SCIMAT or bibliometrix (Aria & Cuccurullo, 2017).

We aim to give an idea of the complexity behind bibliometrics that brings several unanswered questions: an overview of the Journal of Informetrics would help to understand that academic debate on this issue is alive. Instead, our aim is to provide an overview of the ongoing discussion that is less formal than the one happening in an academic journal, but it offers useful insights for young researchers.

Table 5.1 Bibliometric analysis (our elaboration from Cobo et al., 2011a)

			Co-Author	*Co-Citation*	*Co-word*	*Bibliographic coupling*
Unit of Analysis	Author	Name	✓			
		International positioning/relevance				✓
		Reference		✓		
	Journal	International positioning/relevance				✓
		Reference		✓		
	Country of origin	Affiliation	✓			
		Institution	✓			
	In the text	Keywords/terms			✓	
		References		✓		
Sources		Author	✓	✓		✓
		Document	✓	✓	✓	✓
		Journal	✓	✓		✓
Kind of relation		Common references among author's oeuvres				✓
		Common references among documents				✓
		Common references among journal's oeuvre				✓
		Authors' co-occurrence	✓			
		Countries' co-occurrence	✓			
		Institutions' co-occurrence	✓			
		Co-cited author		✓		
		Co-cited documents and journals		✓		
		Terms' co-occurrence			✓	
		Co-cited journal				

Some blogs give suggestions about informetrics and science mapping. Few blogs run by librarians[1] offer an overview of free science mapping tools. In other cases, universities develop blogs to inform about research activity.[2] The promotion of bibliometric research is often linked to the availability of specific programmes or software internally designed by faculty researchers.

As we can see, the world of bibliometrics is extraordinarily dynamic, and there is a variety of motivations that influence its development.

Some Critical Issues

Bibliometrics has many positive aspects: citations can help in providing information about the relevance of a paper. The availability of open access articles, the proliferation of academic journals and the growing number of conferences organized at a global level create the conditions for a considerable number of publications.

The growth of the number of organized conferences facilitates the chance of publishing papers and make them available on the web.

We have searched how many conferences on entrepreneurship take place every year. Our attention was hit by an open science research organisation entitled the World Academy of Science, Engineering and Technology (or WASET) that organizes conferences which topics range from agrometeorology to zoology. WASET has scheduled more than 280 conferences on entrepreneurship in 2020.[3] Conference papers can be published in the meeting organisation journal. As we can read from the website: "all submitted articles are peer-reviewed within approximately three months of submission and accepted full-text articles are published on the Internet, free-of-charge, at no charge (no article processing charges) to authors, as soon as the final versions of articles are received" (https://publications.waset.org). Articles are indexed, and their accessibility ensures notable impact factor: according to the data released by

[1] The following blog represents an example of blogs run by librarians: http://musingsaboutlibrarianship.blogspot.com.

[2] https://researchblog.duke.edu/2018/02/06/duke-scholars-bridge-disciplines-to-tackle-big-questions/ or https://www.cwts.nl/blog?article=n-r2x284&title=mapping-science-using-microsoft-academic-data.

[3] For a detailed list, please visit https://waset.org/entrepreneurship-conferences.

the association, WASET online publications have achieved on the Open Science Citation Index a 3,436 score.

We agree with the necessity of making information and research accessible, but we share the concerns that emerge from the article by Stephan, Veugelers, and Wang (2017). The authors have published a very intriguing piece on Nature in 2017 entitled "Reviewers are blinkered by bibliometrics". In the article, the scholars describe a mechanism that aims to ensure the quality of published papers but that—simultaneously—has stimulated some controversial publishing dynamics. Bibliometric indicators can play a role in hiring and promotions, and the authors cite the cases of Spain, where the salary increase based on productivity depends on JIFs (journal impact factor), or Italy, USA or China. Also, grants and funding assignments can be influenced by the relevance of scholars: "Public funders use these measures to allocate resources to universities. In turn, universities use them to distribute resources to departments" (p. 412). We understand that, if there is a system that promotes massive employment of JIF when making decisions, then the attention of scholars focuses on how to get the most from their publications.

The relationship associating JIF to quality of the publication is at the centre of the academic debate.

This happens even because there are many ways for increasing the rating of a journal. Publishing reviews is a way for improving citations (Pontille & Torny, 2010); reviewers who request authors to cite additional papers published in the same journals can improve journal impact factor (Agrawal, 2005).

We have briefly outlined some critical issues that emerge from the debate on the quality of publications and impact factors. We aimed to underline pros and cons in bibliometrics. To our knowledge, an excessive focus on bibliometrics can represent a limitation.

The Extent of Niches

In our research, we have highlighted that the topic of good entrepreneurs finds articulation in niches, and we have explored the academic contributions to each item.

Our research questions are: Which is the dimension of niches? What are the boundaries of each topic? Where are articles published? Which areas does each topic cover? What type of scholars do they attract and involve?

Following our questions, we have conducted a literature review.

The work by Benavides-Velasco, Quintana-García, and Guzmán-Parra (2013) provides adequate insights for the design of the methodology for this literature review.

Other useful inputs emerge from the work by Paré (2017). In conducting our review, we aimed to propose a map of the existing literature. At the same time, we wanted to analyse the range and the nature of research activities in particular areas, to highlight research gaps in the existing literature and trends. Therefore, our work can't be defined neither as a mapping nor a *scoping review*. We should also consider another important issue: grey literature is growing. With referral to some of the keywords we have employed for database search—for instance, ecopreneur or enviropreneur, as we will see later—search results differ between web (Google Scholar) and academic databases.

The difference between the sources of information is impressive. There is a multitude of articles accessible on the web through academic networks: Researchgate and Academia provide a high quantity of papers in general. For what concerns the coverage of selected themes, Academia, for example, collects 268 documents that deal with the topic of ecopreneurship; Researchgate shows more than 50 results of works concerning ecopreneurship; WOS, on the other hand, includes only nine published articles. Academic networks provide a multitude of sources: articles, book reviews, dissertations, working papers or green papers. Then, academic web-based networks include a myriad of profiles: there are professors, professionals, PhD candidates but also graduate or undergraduate students. All the members of web-based academic networks can upload their publications—without asking for a review—and share with the other members. Publications appear in web search results (Google Scholar among the others), but there is no information about the author's profile. Although emerging insights from grey literature appear extremely interesting, we have decided to perform an analysis of output emerging from academic publishing search engines. Grey literature includes articles not formally published by commercial, academic publishers (Haddaway, Collins, Coughlin, & Kirk, 2015).

We have performed a search on the Web of Science database. We have implemented a keywords-based search, and we have examined where the keywords appear as a topic among published articles. Then, by using the report analysis tool, we have collected information according to the following issues: WOS categories, research areas, countries/regions, publication years and language.

According to the collected information, we can have an idea of the degree of research concentration and the research areas of interest.

The theme of **social entrepreneurship** is vast. Our research focuses on 11.643 records, whose majority (the 29,949%) belongs to the WOS category business; another 24,384% belongs to management and 10,753% to economics.

There are a full number of WOS categories which show interest in social entrepreneurship. Many publications explore the topic of social entrepreneurship in history (2.199% or 256 published articles), regional urban planning (348 or 2.989%), social issues, public administration and so forth. From an analysis of research areas, we can say that the field of business economics is the most active area. The emerging characteristics of social entrepreneurs that we have previously outlined motivate the interest by agriculture or anthropology.

English is the most employed language since it represents the primary language for academic journals. We also have other languages, such as Portuguese, Serbian and French, that find a significant diffusion among scholars.

We can make similar considerations for the topic of **sustainable entrepreneurship**. From the analysis of WOS results, it emerges that most of the publication (95.126%) is in English. Besides the leading role of the USA in the development of this niche (13.093% of the results belong to US scholars), China plays a pivotal role in its growth (8.483% out of the total of results). 45.68% of the results belong to the "business economics" research area, while 21% belongs to environmental science and technology. There is a fragmentation of the results, according to the research area they belong: we can find publications that explore the topic of sustainable entrepreneurship in many categories, from government law to food science, technology and psychology.

In general, we can say that, except for a concentration in business, we can see that publication activity is spread among different categories. The employment of some specific words such as ecopreneur is still limited in published articles: general terms such as social or green entrepreneur show a wider diffusion (Table 5.2).

There is another niche of very impressive dimensions: **green entrepreneurship**. As we can image, the niches of **enviropreneurship** and **ecopreneurship** are quite small: the words employed are precise, so

Table 5.2 Articles by WOS typology (our Elaboration)

	Social entrepreneurship		*Green Entrepreneur*		*Enviropreneur*		*Ecopreneur*		*Sustainable Ecopreneur*	
Web of science categories	*records*	*% of 11643*	*records*	*% of 489*	*records*	*% of 489*	*records*	*% of 9*	*records*	*% of 3796*
Agricultural economics policy									56	1.475
Anthropology	165	1.417								
Area of studies	246	2.113	10	2.045					943	24.842
Business	3487	29.949	120	24.540	5	33.333	5	55.556	83	2.187
Business finance	122	1.048			1	6.667				
Applied chemistry					1	6.667				
Communication	158	1.357							55	1.449
Computer science information systems			6	1.227						
Computer science interdisciplinary applications									48	1.264
Development studies	389	3.341	21	4.294					92	2.424
Ecology			9	1.840						
Economics	1252	10.753	53	10.838					484	12.750
Education educational research	440	3.779	6	1.227					270	7.113
Education scientific disciplines									52	1.370
Energy fuels			9	1.840	1	6.667			64	1.686
Engineering environmental			30	6.135	1	6.667			55	1.449

(continued)

Table 5.2 (continued)

	Social entrepreneurship		*Green Entrepreneur*		*Enviropreneur*		*Ecopreneur*		*Sustainable Ecopreneur*	
Web of science categories	*records*	*% of 11643*	*records*	*% of 489*	*records*	*% of 489*	*records*	*% of 9*	*records*	*% of 3796*
Environmental sciences	412	3.539	93	19.018	4	26.667	2	22.222	134	3.530
Engineering industrial									61	1.607
Engineering (multidisciplinary)									55	1.449
Environmental sciences									565	14.884
Environmental studies	697	5.986	107	21.881	1	6.667	3	33.333	565	14.884
Ethics	203	1.744	5	1.022						
Forestry			8	1.636						
Geography	499	4.286	31	6.339					104	2.740
Green sustainable science technology	367	3.152	84	17.178	3	20.000			564	14.858
History	256	2.199	5	1.022						
Hospitality leisure sport tourism	265	2.276	12	2.454					137	3.609
Information science library science	145	1.245								23.999
International relations			9	1.840						1.317

	Social entrepreneurship		*Green Entrepreneur*		*Enviropreneur*		*Ecopreneur*		*Sustainable Ecopreneur*	
Web of science categories	*records*	*% of 11643*	*records*	*% of 489*	*records*	*% of 489*	*records*	*% of 9*	*records*	*% of 3796*
Management	2839	24.384	99	20.245	3	20.000	4	44.444	911	2.134
Materials science (multidisciplinary)					1	6.667				5.848
Multidisciplinary sciences			8	1.636	1	6.667			50	4.426
Operations research management science									81	1.607
Political science	295	2.534	14	2.863						
Psychology (applied)	140	1.202			1	6.667				
Public administration	248	2.130								
Regional urban planning	348	2.989	28	5.726	1	6.667			222	5.848
Social issues	199	1.709	6	1.227						
Social sciences (interdisciplinary)	444	3.813			1	6.667			168	4.426
Sociology	653	5.609	6	1.227						
Urban studies	261	2.242	18	3.681					61	1.607

the publication strategy is focused. Authors tend to publish in journals that belong to business, management or environmental focused area of study.

When we examine the distribution of publications by year, we can see how the interest in the mentioned topics has evolved. Figure 5.1 shows the distribution of articles by year. We must underline that the collected information about 2020 does not cover the entire year and is limited to the period January–May; in any case, they provide useful insights about the trends of topics and academic publications.

The interest for the selected topics grows on a yearly base and reached its pick in 2019 (Fig. 5.1). Due to the vastity of the theme, social entrepreneurship plays the main role in research development, but also green entrepreneurship has found an expansion in the last years.

The geographical diffusion of the interest among countries emerges from the analysis of scholars' affiliations. US scholars have published almost 25% of the total of articles on social entrepreneurship and released in the period 1960–2020. England, Spain and Canada cover respectively the 13.41, 6.96 and 5.67 of the total of published articles that cover the topic of social entrepreneurship.

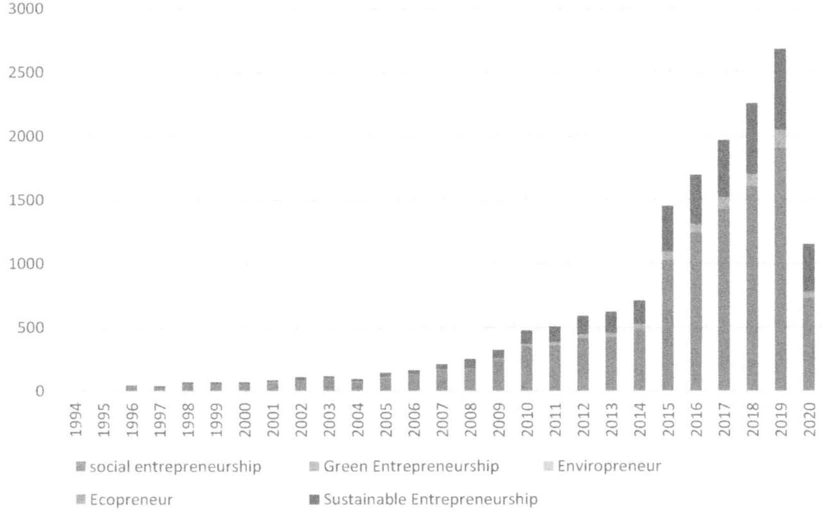

Fig. 5.1 Publications by year

For what concerns green entrepreneurship, we see that the USA leads scholarly publications (18%); then, we notice an intense concentration of scholars from the UK and China.

We also see a diffused interest among European scholars for these themes: more specifically northern Europe (Germany, Sweden Norway) shows interest in following green and social entrepreneurship.

We can finally make some comments on the collected information.

First of all, we can say that if specific terminology grows, also the focus of publication grows. In other words, scholars who employ particular terms are more likely to publish on selected journals or areas. Neologism and new issues find a wide diffusion in unconventional publications. Grey literature that is not strictly linked to academic standards is amorphous and has a variety of purposes (Haddaway et al., 2015) and could play a leading role in bringing some new themes, or concepts, to the spotlight. Some research (Haddaway et al., 2015) shows that in some cases the overlapping between Google Scholar results and WOS is extremely low and the combination of the emerging results of both databases can be useful for increasing the coverage of any multi-database search, especially for systematic reviews (Haddaway et al., 2015).

Grey Literature

Yet, grey literature shows some limits. The most relevant problem with grey literature is that there is a lack of peer review. Recently, scholars have outlined that also grey literature can vary according to the degree of "reliability" of the published articles. From the combination of the knowledgeability of source expertise and outlet control, we obtain different "greys" for the literature that can have low or significant retrievability or credibility (Adams, Smart, & Huff, 2017). Grey literature is an unavoidable phenomenon that is supposed to gain importance since we see that info sources are increasing together with the variety of available materials. The work by Adams et al. (2017) provides a comprehensive list of the different types of documents that can be found on the web. Those who seek information about some topics can choose among various types of papers (discussion papers, white papers, green papers or version of draft papers whose final version is then published on academic journals or rejected manuscripts), publications from governmental agencies or companies, technical notes, newsletters, reports (that can be programme evaluation reports or company reports, among the others), speeches or conference abstracts. As we can see the source of information is impressive, and scholars must accurately choose inputs and evaluate their relevancy for their research activity.

We have carried out a little research on Google Scholar to evaluate the role that grey literature could have in the study of niches in "good entrepreneurship".

Since its introduction in 2004, Google Scholar (or GS) has revolutionized the world of citations. Some researches have focused on the degree of overlapping between GS and other databases, such as WOS (see among the others De Winter, Zadpoor, and Dodou (2014)); given its accessibility, GS has found ample employment (Halevi, Moed, & Bar-Ilan, 2017), but scholars recommend not to use it alone and underline that it is not a replacement for academic citation databases (Haddaway et al., 2015). GS is particularly helpful for students, and recent studies have confirmed that its usage fostered the students' degree of information literacy (Mikki, 2009).

We have performed an analysis of GS results following the insights emerging from the literature (De Winter et al., 2014; Haddaway et al., 2015; Mikki, 2009). We aimed to evaluate the diffusion of documents that deal with the topics of social, green eco and environmental entrepreneurship. We have selected the same keywords used for the WOS analysis, and the results are summarized in (Fig. 5.2).

The analysis of the number of articles published in 2020 is limited to the period of January–July 2020.

Each group of data covers five years, with an exception for the first group that covers the period 1950–1990. We have decided to extend the research to a broader period in the first group, because, in general, the number of articles dedicated to the selected topics was scarce before the 1990s. Therefore, in order to have a better representation of data, we have included more of them in the first group.

We can see that the number of publications grows year by year. Some topics show a wider diffusion. It is the case of social entrepreneurship, sustainable entrepreneurship and green entrepreneurship. The other two items, ecopreneurship and enviropreneurship, have been lately introduced and their diffusion is not as wide as the other two. Yet, they are growing by the number of publications. Ecopreneurship, for example, in the last five years has reached a pick of 99 items on Google Scholar, and they were only 50 just five years before. We can see a similar trend for enviropreneur.

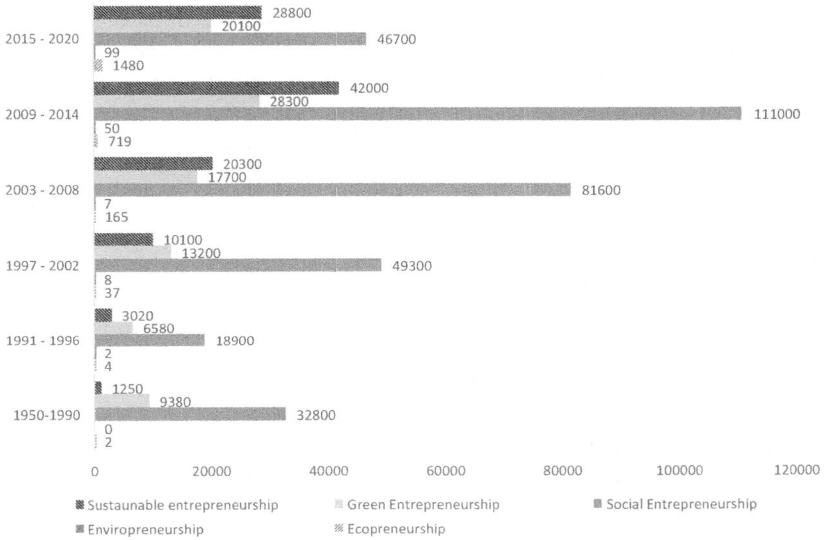

Fig. 5.2 Google Scholar analysis

The numbers are impressive for social entrepreneurship: as we have previously outlined, the issue of social entrepreneurship has found a wide diffusion since its first appearance on the academic scene. If we observe more in detail the period 1950–1990, we can see that 9% of the total of publications is referred to the first decade (1950–1960). Then, the other decades account respectively for 17, 32 and 43% of the total publications in the entire considered period.

Publications grow, given the interest for some thematic issues—from community engagement to welfare or sustainability—that appear pivotal for economic development.

Research Life Cycle

We have previously outlined the different phases that a research field encounters in its journey, from its birth to the challenges of achieving legitimacy among scholars. We know that many elements foster the development of a research field.

In particular, we know that the interest that some groups of people—professionals, associations, institutions, policymakers—show towards some thematic issues can act as an attractor for funding and economic resources. It also appears that publishing strategies are affected by a multitude of factors that range from scholars' bibliographic search strategy to JIF.

Given the development of grey literature, we can suggest to connect the dynamics that influence grey literature to those that characterise "standard" literature.

Scholars have paid much attention in understanding the role of grey literature in reducing literature review bias: the study conducted by Hopewell, Clarke, and Mallett (2005), although focusing on health science, clearly depicts how scholars can employ grey literature in their search strategy to achieve a comprehensive overview of academic contributions in a defined field. This is particularly true for those research fields where some documents, such as conference papers, provide useful and innovative insights.

In our opinion, we should change the approach to literature: from a development based on quantitative indicators (number of publications, number of citations), we should try to understand how a research field evolves over time.

We have developed a sort of model that explains the progress that research niches can have.

In the first stage, the theme is introduced; the number of publications is relatively small and capable to attract fewer scholars. Most of the contributions can come from grey literature.

As the number of published articles grows, grey literature can turn into white literature.

We are borrowing the metaphor, the shift from grey to white, from an inspiring article published by de Blaaij (2004) who compares the evolution of the role of grey literature to the evolution of Gandalf in The Two Towers, from the trilogy "Lord of The Rings": the evolution was pivotal for further development of the story. Similarly, when literature from grey becomes white, the topic becomes more accessible and visible.

Our preliminary research suggests that when an issue gets a notable diffusion in the grey literature, it can become an exciting theme in the white literature, and it achieves a degree of notoriety among scholars. After the introduction, a research issue can register a speed growth, due to the presence of incentives that stimulate its growth. These incentives can be various: from the engagement of the academic community to the interest shown by institutions. Some drivers stimulate articles proliferation; among the others, we can include in this list the availability of niche-focused research conference sessions, special issues dedicated by journals or funding opportunities. The growth can be associated with an introduction of the research niche in the white literature, which contribution is limited at a first phase, but increasing in a second phase. Research niche will reach a maturity stage that combines a peak in the number of publications with a legitimation of the niche.

Then, the curve of the life cycle can decline or it can remain stable. If the research theme achieves a high consideration among scholars, the number of publications remains stable or can have a slight decrease. This means that from niche, the research then came to upstream. Then, the research issue can have a revitalisation. It can generate, for instance, other research niches. This is what has happened to the vast issue of green entrepreneurship that has seen smaller niches grow, such as ecopreneurship or enviropreneurship.

Then, another niche cycle starts, and a new process takes places.

Some Final Remarks

As we can see, the topic of the research niche is exceptionally dynamic. With a specific referral to the subject of good entrepreneur, we can see that new niches were born and research registered signs of progress.

The phases that regulate a life cycle are the introduction; the growth phase; the maturity; and the decline. Starting from the general principle that emerges from the theory of product lifecycle management and niches, we can make some final considerations.

We have seen that some research niches were born in the field of entrepreneurship, and their width varies: the adoption of general terminology to define research theme promotes a broad interest for the topic and its diffusion. This also leads to publishing in various research areas and journals.

Inside broader research topics, smaller research issues arise when the main topic reaches a considerable diffusion among academicians; this creates the opportunities for niching down the areas which publication aims are tailored on specific journals and audience.

Therefore, we have seen that grey literature supports the growth of some smaller research niches, and it represents a way for promoting new approaches to some selected research topics or some specific research issues. After having created an adequate awareness towards the research theme, academicians seek for publications in academic journals. Under this perspective, grey literature represents a tool for monitoring research progress and developments.

We can see that in the development of a research niche, many elements coexist: authors strategically manage publication choices and seek for a general consensus. Grey literature can help to create interest in niche research issues, but also to increase academicians' personal notoriety. It can also represent a way for shortening the "introduction" phase in the life cycle of a research niche: during the introduction of the research theme in the academic environment, authors aim to make a topic relevant for scholars and to foster debate. Grey literature ensures the availability of research outcomes on the web, and the timing is shorter if compared to the "traditional" publication system; at the same time, grey literature is, for its majority, open access, and therefore, it promotes the circulation of research output.

In this final paragraph, we have decided to include a set of graphs that illustrate the evolution of publications by number over time. We can see how the curve of scholar results anticipates the growth of WOS results. Yet, it is still too early to make forecasts about the degree of maturity of each niche. We can say that, where the degree of specificity of the research issue is particularly high, we notice that the values of Scholar and WOS show tremendous differences by numbers.

We also have to remember that 2020 data don't cover the full year. For the future, we can suppose that grey literature will see a reduction in its growth rate, while traditional publication will grow. The recognition of a niche research field, as a legitimate research theme, could nurture scholars' interest for the topic. Still, it is hard to say if we will ever see traditional literature have higher growth rate than grey literature. It is also hard to say if we will see new niches emerging.

We are sure that the topic of doing the good and the study of the different categories of entrepreneurs is growing and there is enough space for new research approaches and field research (Figs. 5.3, 5.4, 5.5, 5.6 and 5.7).

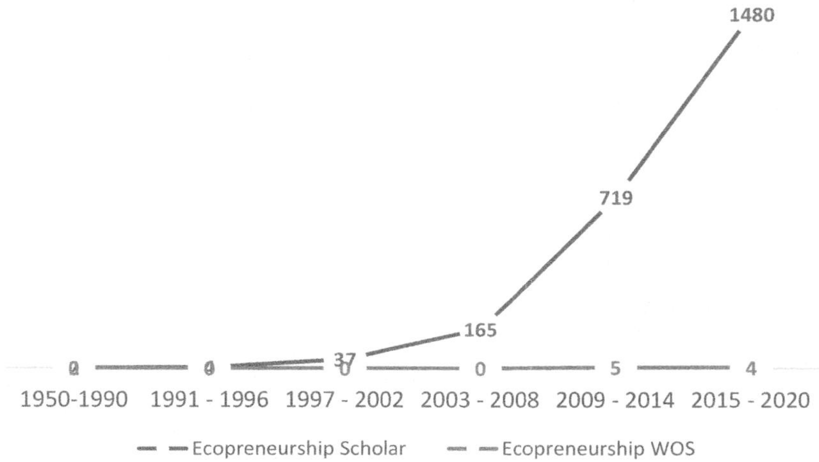

Fig. 5.3 Ecopreneurship

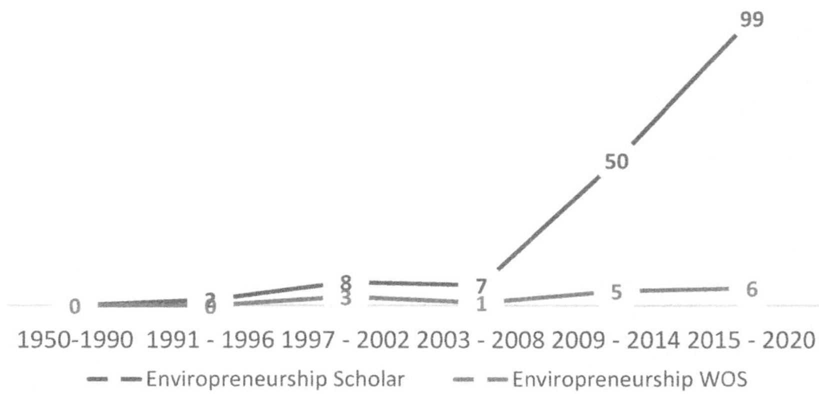

Fig. 5.4 Enviropreneurship

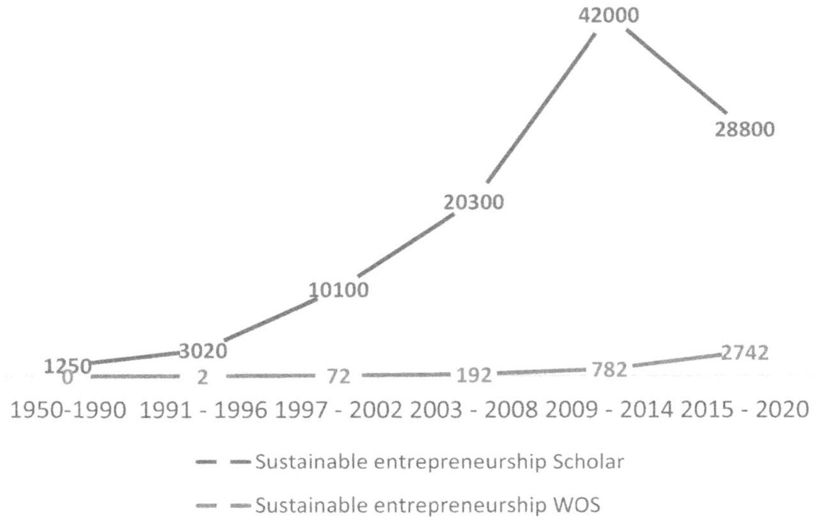

Fig. 5.5 Sustainable Entrepreneurship

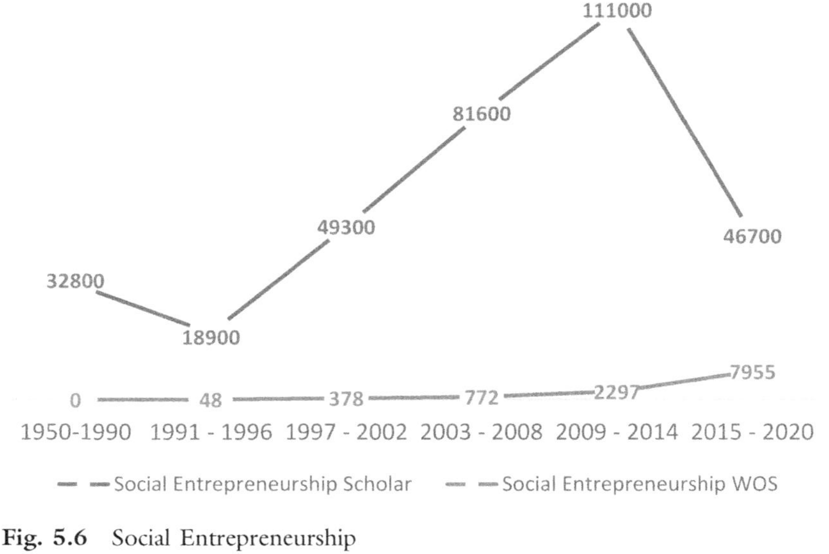

Fig. 5.6 Social Entrepreneurship

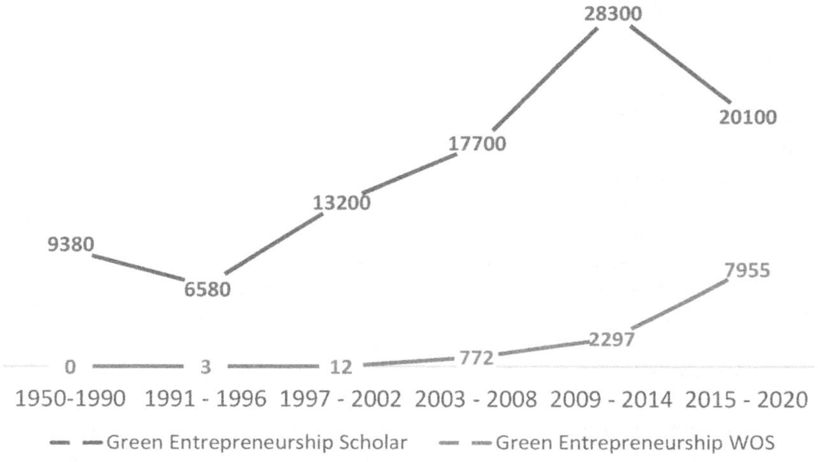

Fig. 5.7 Green Entrepreneurship

References

Adams, R. J., Smart, P., & Huff, A. S. (2017). Shades of grey: Guidelines for working with the grey literature in systematic reviews for management and organizational studies. *International Journal of Management Reviews, 9*(4), 432–454.

Agrawal, A. (2005). Corruption of journal impact factors. *Trends in Ecology & Evolution, 20,* 157.

Aria, M., & Cuccurullo, C. (2017). Bibliometrix: An R-tool for comprehensive science mapping analysis. *Journal of Informetrics, 11*(4), 959–975. https://doi.org/10.1016/j.joi.2017.08.007.

Benavides-Velasco, C. A., Quintana-García, C., & Guzmán-Parra, V. F. (2013). Trends in family business research. *Small Business Economics, 40*(1), 41–57.

Cobo, M. J., López-Herrera, A. G., Herrera-Viedma, E., & Herrera, F. (2011a). An approach for detecting, quantifying, and visualizing the evolution of a research field: A practical application to the Fuzzy Sets Theory field. *Journal of Informetrics, 5*(1), 146–166.

Cobo, M. J., López-Herrera, A. G., Herrera-Viedma, E., & Herrera, F. (2011b). Science mapping software tools: Review, analysis, and cooperative study among tools. *Journal of the American Society for Information Science and Technology, 62*(7), 1382–1402.

de Blaaij, C. (2004). Grey literature from invisibility to visibility. *Publishing Research Quarterly, 20*(1), 70–76.

De Winter, J. C., Zadpoor, A. A., & Dodou, D. (2014). The expansion of google scholar versus web of science: A longitudinal study. *Scientometrics, 98*(2), 1547–1565.

Haddaway, N., Collins, A., Coughlin, D., & Kirk, S. (2015). The role of google scholar in evidence reviews and its applicability to grey literature searching. *PLoS ONE, 10*(9).

Halevi, G., Moed, H., & Bar-Ilan, J. (2017). Suitability of google scholar as a source of scientific information and as a source of data for scientific evaluation—Review of the literature. *Journal of Informetrics, 11(3)*, 823–834.

Hopewell, S., Clarke, M., & Mallett, S. (2005). Grey literature and systematic reviews. In H. R. Rothstein, A. J. Sutton, & M. Borenstein (Eds.), *Publication bias in meta-analysis: Prevention, assessment and adjustments* (pp. 49–72). Springer.

Mikki, S. (2009). Google scholar compared to web of science. A literature review. *Nordic Journal of Information Literacy in Higher Education, 1*(1), 41–51.

Paré G, K. S. (2017). Methods for literature reviews. In F. Lau & C. Kuziemsky (Eds.), *Handbook of ehealth evaluation: An evidence-based approach*. Retrieved from https://www.ncbi.nlm.nih.gov/books/NBK481583/.

Pontille, D., & Torny, D. (2010). The controversial policies of journal ratings: Evaluating social sciences and humanities. *Research Evaluation, 19*(5), 347–360.

Rocco, T. S., & Plakhotnik, M. S. (2009). Literature reviews, conceptual frameworks, and theoretical frameworks: Terms, functions, and distinctions. *Human Resource Development Review, 8*(1), 120–130.

Stephan, P., Veugelers, R., & Wang, J. (2017). Reviewers are blinkered by bibliometrics. *Nature, 544*(7651), 411–412.

Conclusion

The idea of focusing on the good entrepreneur came to my mind by observing reality. I have encountered many entrepreneurs during my researches, and I come from an industrial district, in central Italy, that is famous all over the world for its textile production. In my hometown, Prato, people are facing a global crisis, and for small companies, it is tough to survive. I have learned that entrepreneurs have a risk-taking attitude; they are capable of seizing opportunities and of recognising a chance where most of the people don't see anything.

I belong to a generation—GenX—that has to take societal and environmental problems in serious consideration. I have had the chance to observe some solitary and independent entrepreneurs, often depicted as illuminated heroes.

As many other scholars, I have suddenly recognized that entrepreneurs who were focusing on "doing the good" were growing.

Since the beginning, as it emerges from the earliest literature, entrepreneurs were animated by the need for changing and for creating opportunities. They contribute to the economic well-being of the local communities, by creating jobs and by improving the culture of entrepreneurship.

Thus, the need for doing the good gained much space in the entrepreneurial decision process.

In my opinion, from the analysis of the literature, we can see some significant steps that led to new types of entrepreneurship.

C. Santini, *The Good Entrepreneur*,
https://doi.org/10.1007/978-3-030-59332-2

The debate on doing well by doing good or doing well and doing good represents the starting point of the process. Initially, the problem was to decide between pursuing profits or the good.

Then, with the progress in corporate social responsibility and the implementation of sustainable and environmental practices, ethical motives in entrepreneurial behaviour gained more space also in academic research.

Scholars must combine several aims: on the one hand, they have to focus on research issues that are capable of attracting people's interest; on the other, they have to face some "practical" challenges. Scholars have to keep an eye on the financial sustainability of their activities: carrying out researches also means dealing with a budget and expenses; therefore, it is essential to find out people who might be interested in financing the study or having the chance to apply for funding.

At the same time, scholars also need to elaborate a publishing strategy. We have seen how many factors influence the systems of publishing decisions. As it emerges from the discussion on the legitimacy of entrepreneurship as a research field, there is also a link between the recognition of the importance of a research field, and its academic legitimacy and the emerging of scholarly debate on the topic. Yet, it is also essential to notice that as the number of publications grows, the theoretical discussion improves.

Research in entrepreneurship is fragmented; thus, research niches are different from fragments: we have seen how niches evolve. We think that the emerging of research niches is supported by the rising of the phenomenon of grey literature. As we have seen, grey literature had the merit of bringing under the spotlight some issues that deal with a particular aspect of entrepreneurship. Grey literature attracts scholars, not only because it represents a source of information and visibility, but also because it has influenced the publishing dynamics in Academia.

In this scenario, grey literature represents a valuable input for the development of research niches.

Good entrepreneurship is a hot topic, and it is attracting scholars' attention: as a global society, we are experiencing a time of change, with the urgency of having a comprehensive overview of stakeholders' needs. Research has the arduous duty to elaborate general concernments for environment, society, welfare and well-being; to help build solutions; or to provide inspirations to professionals. The literature has plenty of cases, examples, even if one of the limits of the research in emerging niches is the lack in field works: taxonomies, classifications and theoretical works are abundant, so scholars complain about the lack of field research. Thus, this is the typical situation that characterizes research niches in their early stages.

Therefore, scholars who can communicate the insights of their research to professionals and other stakeholders (e.g. policymakers) can have an active role in contributing to solve some problems affecting society and communities.

It is vital to observe the dynamics that characterize good entrepreneurs: the understanding of what facilitates entrepreneurs in pursuing the good can help policymakers and institutions to elaborate strategies that support good entrepreneurial behaviours. We have seen that the active involvement of green, social, environmental or sustainable entrepreneur was a valuable help in critical situations, such as disaster recovering and management. We have also seen that social entrepreneurs are taken into significant consideration for the development of a welfare system.

Therefore, we have analysed the issue of good entrepreneurship from a twofold perspective. On one side, we have analysed the characteristics of good entrepreneurs, as they emerge from the scholars' observation of reality. On the other, we have tried to understand the motives of scholars' interest in this research issue, the theoretical debate and the trends in publishing and research. This second perspective is mainly theoretical, and it outlines some dynamics of the academic environment. In the book, we have tried to describe the process that makes a topic "interesting" for scholars. Today universities have a leading role in the promotion of good practices among entrepreneurs. Therefore, making research more accessible to different stakeholders can represent a significant step. Good entrepreneurs have a leading role within the society: we have assisted to the birth of new types of entrepreneurs, and in future, new niches are expected to rise. We have also seen that the "doing well or doing good" dichotomy is an old problem: we have seen that the profit and good perspective can coexist. The multitude of solutions provided by good entrepreneurs has created a lively scenario that opens to many research questions about new forms of business, new types of entrepreneurs and the impact that social and community factors can have on the shaping of entrepreneurial behaviour.

Consequently, a researcher engaged with the reality has a multitude of questions: which publishing strategy to choose according to the personal aims; what is the contribution that academicians can give to good entrepreneurs and local stakeholders; and so forth.

This book was intended to stimulate a reflection upon the topic of good in entrepreneurship, but also on the role that academicians can have when approaching this issue. We hope to have succeeded in our primary scope.

Index

C. Santini, *The Good Entrepreneur*,
https://doi.org/10.1007/978-3-030-59332-2